A BOOK OF SAINTS

A BOOK
OF SAINTS

True Stories of How They
Touch Our Lives

Anne Gordon

BANTAM BOOKS
New York   Toronto   London   Sydney   Auckland

A BOOK OF SAINTS
A Bantam Book / August 1994

Art on pages ii and iii: Christ and a procession of saints
and martyrs. (Denver Art Museum)
Art on part opening pages: Assembly of Saints.

65189

Book design by Maria Carella

Library of Congress Cataloging-in-Publication Data

Gordon, Anne, 1956–
    A book of saints : true stories of how they touch our lives / by
Anne Gordon.
        p.   cm.
    Includes bibliographical references and index.
    ISBN 0-553-37272-6
    1. Christian saints.   2. Spiritual life—Christianity.   I. Title.
  Bx4655.2.G67   1994
282'.092'2—dc20
[B]   93-39437
                                                  CIP

Published simultaneously in the United States and Canada

Bantam Books are published by Bantam Books, a division of Bantam Doubleday Dell Publishing
Group, Inc. Its trademark, consisting of the words "Bantam Books" and the portrayal of a rooster,
is Registered in U.S. Patent and Trademark Office and in other countries. Marca Registrada. Bantam
Books, 1540 Broadway, New York, New York 10036.

PRINTED IN THE UNITED STATES OF AMERICA

FFG   0 9 8 7 6 5 4 3 2 1

In memory of
Ken Gordon
and Channa Rose Berman

A man dies as he dies. Only the saint chooses his death as he has chosen his life; is the master of his coming and going.

—RAMON GUTHRIE

CONTENTS

PART THREE
LESSONS OF THE SAINTS

LIST OF ILLUSTRATIONS

INTRODUCTION

—◈—

*F*our years ago, I was struck by tragedy. My younger brother, Kenny, died at the age of thirty. I felt pain and sorrow and had many a twisting, sleepless night, but most of all I just wanted to know if he was finally free from pain. Where is he? I wondered. And how might I reach him to see if he is all right? More than ever before I wanted to know about the afterlife and prayer.

Not long after my brother's death, I began praying earnestly to God, but somehow He seemed too distant, too unreachable for me. I soon realized that I needed the human touch to aid me in my attempts to bridge the gap between heaven and earth. In a quest to rekindle my faith, I turned to the saints for help. The book you hold in your hands is the result of this effort to reach out to the saints for a new sense of meaning and purpose in life.

In addition to "making contact" with the saints, my hope in writing this book has been to organize the many disconnected fragments of my spiritual reflections into a more unified and meaningful whole. I long ago reached the conclusion that unless we are clear about what we do and do not believe—unless we are able to fashion for ourselves a holistic, comprehensive spiritual vision for our lives—it is quite impossible to

live with any degree of depth, conviction, or purpose. The saints seemed the perfect place to turn for assistance in attaining deeper insights into the nature of spiritual truth.

At their truest, I believe that saints are God's elect, not quite supernatural but not quite Everyman, either. While they are men and women like ourselves, they have chosen to model their lives after that of Jesus. They do as Paul exhorted in Ephesians 5:1–2: "Be imitators of God as His dear children." Their lives show us that there is a way to practice the teachings of the Gospel so long as we are willing to devote ourselves to the task of loving service.

The saints sought to imitate Christ with their lives. They hoped to heal other people, and themselves, by living a Christian life rich with meaning. Yet—to one degree or another—each of them had his or her own definition of what it meant to be a spiritual person and how best to exemplify God's message. Today, in a time when the tide runs toward the shore of conformity, when we are constantly hounded by one religious group after another to follow the "one and only path to God," I find it refreshing to know that the saints walked toward God in a wide variety of ways. Through living a life of poverty, Saint Francis revealed his comprehension of what it means to be a Christian. Joan of Arc conveyed her understanding of sanctity through a profound display of patriotism. Saint Anselm reached out to God through studying and interpreting scripture. Saint Patrick found his meaning through evangelism. Saint Kolbe found his through self-sacrifice. All of these saints defined Christianity as unique individuals in distinctly different periods in history.

After working on this book for less than two months, it became clear to me that covering the vast sweep of Christian history and the saints would be an enormous undertaking. My early Catholic education had taught me little about mysticism and contemplative theology, and even less about the role of saints in the history of the Church. I read books on ancient history and scanned theological documents in an effort to grasp the meaning of

The Holy Face of Jesus, as depicted by the great New Mexican santero Rafael Aragon.

(Courtesy of the Harwood Foundation, The University of New Mexico)

the saints' lives and their relevance to us today. I read a great deal of scholarly material because few popular books on saints go beyond mere legend.

Many of the popular so-called biographies I read were nothing more than what scholars call "hagiographies"—highly subjective and frequently factless accounts of the saints composed by men and women blinded by love. Almost invariably these pictures were of morally flawless men and women who performed miracles at will, with no accounts of the more human and less praiseworthy aspects of their life. Saints, after all, are human. Not a single one of them was perfect. Ambrose Bierce understood this well when he humorously wrote that a saint is nothing more than "a dead sinner revised and edited." While the hagiographers tended to forget this, I quickly learned to forgive their exaggerations and fantasy in the quest for goodness. Hagiographers need their saints as I do, to help them bridge the gap between themselves and their God.

While working on this book, I have spent hundreds of hours talking with men and women who pray to the saints for guidance, solace, comfort, and cures in their lives. These conversations, many of which appear in Chapter 2 of this book, are living testaments that the saints live on; that even today, 1,994 years after the birth of Christ, people's lives are still being affected every day, in a thousand different ways, by the human representatives of God on earth—the saints.

Prayer is a powerful instrument. When we pray to the saints, we diminish the forces of evil in the world. Prayer can aid us in healing, mentally and physically. Prayer can help soothe our soul when a death stuns and cripples the laughter in our life. Prayer is an investment of faith, and praying to the saints can bring about positive, dramatic changes in our lives. These true stories of saints and how they touch our lives will show why saints can continue to play an important role in our spiritual well-being.

The people I spoke with are drawn to a wide variety of saints across the great span of Christian history. Some are attracted to ancient martyrs, others to sixteenth-century mystics, still others to modern-day missionaries such as Mother Frances Cabrini. Different times have posed different challenges to Christians over the years, and from those challenges, new paths to meaning have emerged. Given this, it is helpful to gain some appreciation of the historical forces that compelled these people to search for meaning as they did. Accordingly, I have arranged Part Two of this book around five distinct types of saints in Church history—martyrs, hermits, monastics, missionaries, and mystics—and the lessons they have to offer us today. I must confess, however, that the saints I have chosen to profile in Part Three are my personal favorites—men and women whose lives speak to me powerfully across time.

By arranging Part Two around different types of saints, I do not wish to give the impression that I view each of these servants of God as fitting solely into one category. Quite the contrary, some of the greatest mystic saints were also great missionaries, and some of the Church's most prized scholars were also missionaries, martyrs, and contemplatives. I have never been a great believer in categorization, and for saints and saint-making it seems especially inappropriate. In the end, how we chose to define a saint seems far less important than why and how that saint responded to the challenges of spiritual life.

I know that for many secular-minded people the saints are nothing more than a group of bizarre religious extremists. Others who hold some level of faith view them simply as inspiring role models. But for me, saints are heroes. They were eccentric and charming, passive and aggressive, grouchy and mild, warriors and peacemakers; they got hungry, they got angry with God, they battled their egos, and yes, they made mistakes. They were forever asking for forgiveness and always doubting their passage into heaven. They fell from grace and rose again, and each time they vowed to be better. C. S. Lewis once wrote, "The great sinners are made of the very same material as . . . the great saints." I take comfort in reminding myself

Gandhi recognized the immense power of truth. He knew that truth would overcome all injustice and create a new order.

that the very opposite is also true: The great saints are made from the very same material as the great sinners.

We all learn best by example and imitation. Reading and studying the lives of the saints affords us a special opportunity to pattern our lives after the most spiritually gifted men and women who have ever lived. Jesus said He was a model for all to follow. Men and women have followed Buddha, Gandhi, and Mother Teresa of Calcutta for much the same reason: They admire their holiness, gentleness, and true spirit and hope to emulate them.

When just one man follows his God, others will follow. Saint Maximilian Kolbe, a prisoner in Auschwitz, volunteered his life so another could live. He trusted the example of Jesus with a profound depth of faith and courage. He touched and inspired thousands of others to lead a more Christ-like life, to be more compassionate toward others, to honor their fellow human beings. Each of the saints calls us to do the same. They ask us to devote ourselves sincerely to living a life of spiritual compassion.

Statue of Buddha in the Japanese Garden, Golden Gate Park, San Francisco.

As I reflect on my own life, I realize that many people have given me great gifts without my ever knowing it and without my having asked for it. Our spiritual life can be nourished in the same way we savor and build upon the gifts of others, whether it is a lesson in humility, the sharing of a story, or simply the gift of comfort. Some people say they have never seen anyone demonstrate saintly virtues, but you can see them quite regularly if you reflect on the simple acts of kindness and connection that occur in our lives on a daily basis. At the hospital in San Diego where my brother died, social workers, doctors, counselors, and friends of my brother all extended a hand in charity. We need just to look, to open our eyes to the thousands of small acts of human feeling and caring, to be able to see the saints in our lives.

I hope this book will encourage you to pick some favorite saints, for the life of the soul requires spiritual guideposts, lights of sanctity for guidance along the way. (If you would like to see a list of saints, please refer to page 163.) As the late Dr. Albert Schweitzer so elegantly put it, "The older we grow, the more we realize that true power and happiness comes to us only through those who spiritually mean something to us. Whether they are near or far, still alive or dead, we need them if we are to find our way through life. The good we bear within us can be turned into life and action only when they are near to us in spirit." The saints *are* near to us in spirit—we just need to invite them in and give them a chance to work miracles in our lives.

PART ONE
—
BONDS
OF GRACE

1

THE
IMPORTANCE
OF PRAYER

*M*y great-aunt was once befriended—perhaps even saved—by a saint. On September 3, 1955, when her husband of sixteen years died suddenly from a heart attack at the age of forty-two, Rose St. Louis found herself with four children to rear and a tangle of messy financial matters. Yet instead of doubting her faith, instead of becoming bitter with God for taking away her cherished husband so soon, she turned to Him for courage and guidance.

Rose St. Louis's path to God was not a direct route. Like so many other Christians in the history of the Roman Catholic Church, she chose to find her way to God through the aid of a saint. "Saint Joseph was the head of God's family and I had just lost the head of mine, so it seemed appropriate that I turn to him," she told me. "I think that going through life without a spouse and raising four children is incredibly difficult, and Saint Joseph helped me tremendously in making the right decisions and in guiding me through the day-to-day issues so that I could raise my children properly." She told me that without Saint Joseph's supportive presence, she might never have made it. Today, she still prays to Saint Joseph when she needs a warm and compassionate listener. He has become her trusted friend and spiritual guide.

The great mystic Saint Teresa of Ávila also called Saint Joseph her special friend. "I don't recall up to this day ever having petitioned him for anything that he failed to grant," Saint Teresa once said. "It is an amazing thing the great many favors God has granted me through the mediation of this blessed saint, the dangers I was freed from both of body and soul. For with other saints it seems the Lord has given them grace to be of help in one need, whereas with this glorious saint I have experience that he helps in all our needs."

Saint Joseph is just one of the more than four thousand saints to whom men and women have turned for inspiration and guidance in their lives. The veteran publisher and writer William Nichols calls Saint Anthony of Padua his friend. William suffered the loss of his wife, Mariethe, in 1988, but not before her painful four-year struggle with Alzheimer's disease. "Even during the good years," he wrote, "we both had the habit of dropping in at Saint Patrick's Cathedral in New York to talk with Saint Anthony. Mostly, then, it was about immediate problems—lost objects, job problems, selling our place in Vermont, and the like. It was all in fun then. But later on it was different. During the final stage of her illness, I found myself going almost daily to light a candle, and always with the same prayer: 'Please, Saint Anthony, cure her. But if that is not possible, then please take her.' And he did—just at the moment when the worst was about to begin. And now, with Mariethe gone, it is as if I were impelled by some outer force. Almost automatically, I still go and light my candle, and along with my prayer, I actually feel as if I were talking to her—through him. With that comes a wonderful sense of calmness and strength."[1]

Those of us who have lost someone dear understand what William is talking about. Although my brother Ken died four years ago, still I talk with him; still I ask him for guidance when I am unsure which path to take. It is as if invisible but unbreakable strands connect us with those we love and help us breach the barrier between ourselves and our dead loved ones. This same kind of connection and love can also help us overcome

Saint Joseph, the husband of Mary, is the patron saint of Austria, Belgium, Canada, Mexico, Peru, and Vietnam. He is invoked against communism and doubt and his statue is often buried in the lawns of homes for sale to hasten an early closing.
(Michael O'Shaughnessy)

the distance between ourselves and the saints, and between ourselves and our God, binding us together in a communion of faith. But this distance cannot be breached without prayer, for prayer, I believe, is our bridge to the Divine.

Nearly all of the saints have stressed that prayer is the bedrock of spiritual life. Yet many people today seem embarrassed to speak of prayer, perhaps because it implies that we are powerless over certain things—an unacceptable concept in a culture so bent on independence and achieving "personal power." In our secular world, the admission that we pray instantly says that we are weak, that we need help to make it through the day, that we can't stand alone, that we are not "in control" of our lives. These charges are indeed true of those of us who pray, but they are just as true of those who don't. After all, none of us has absolute control over our lives. Each and every creature needs Divine support to survive. We do not control the tides, the winds, the rains, or a single moon or planet in this whirling galaxy. In truth, our life is capricious, vexing, and baffling, and the great saints and mystic seers have all stressed this through the ages. Constant challenge and change are the only things we can count on.

Besides those people who denounce prayer as weakness, others simply never even consider prayer as an option in their headlong pursuit of wealth, beauty, fame, or power. Søren Kierkegaard called this spiritual unconsciousness "tranquilization by the trivial," and our world is full of a wide array of "trivial pursuits." Advertisers work overtime to keep us tranquilized, to keep us from meditation, contemplation, and prayer; to keep us from recognizing that we really do not need a new car, new drapes, a new home, a new face, or a trip to Paris to find a deeper sense of meaning and purpose in our lives.

Father Henri Nouwen, one of the most thoughtful of contemporary religious writers, suggests another reason why prayer is so difficult for people to practice and express:

Prayer is like incense rising to heaven and draws exhilarating graces from heaven. It strengthens the strayed soul, giving it back peace and calm.
—MOTHER FRANCES CABRINI

What is closest to our person is most difficult to express and explain. This is not just true for lovers, artists and tightrope walkers but also for those who pray. While prayer is the expression of a most intimate relationship, it is also the most difficult subject to speak about and becomes easily the subject of trivialities and platitudes. While it is the most human of all human acts, it is also easily perceived as the most superfluous and superstitious activity.

Yet despite this awkwardness, we *must* talk about prayer. Spiritual life is impossible without it. Through prayer we forge our links with God and His saints to find a bright spiritual vision to illuminate our paths.

Nearly all of the saints have emphatically said that prayer is the fundamental relationship of men and women to God. "In prayer," wrote the nineteenth-century Russian recluse Bishop Theophan, "the principal thing is to stand before God with the mind and the heart, and to go on standing before Him unceasingly day and night until the end of life." In the fourteenth century Saint Gregory of Sinai wrote, "Prayer is God who works all things in all men." I take this to mean that the highest form of prayer is the manifestation of God's grace within us.

Prayer, then, is a gift, not a pursuit. The purpose of prayer is to get nearer to God, for the closer we are to Him, the more spiritually nourished we become. When we are close to God, happiness floods our being. Yet if we were to pursue this closeness with God in an effort to be happy, we not only wouldn't get near Him, we wouldn't find happiness. Happiness is based solely upon our willingness to turn ourselves over to the Divine, to say with utter sincerity, "Thy will be done." To say that and mean it opens the doorway to spiritual bliss. It is also the key to understanding the saints, for they agree that the highest form of prayer is characterized less by pleas for help than by the humble request for clarity of vision and spiritual guidance to help us cope with the difficult and constantly emerging challenges of daily life.

The power of prayer is indeed wonderful. It is like a queen, who having free access always to the king, can obtain whatever she asks. To secure a hearing there is no need to recite set prayers composed for the occasion—were this the case, I should indeed deserve to be pitied!
—SAINT TERESA OF
LISIEUX

The great saints have offered many ways to pray. For the intellectual monastics of the seventeenth century, prayer was structured and rigorous, requiring the recitation of long prayers at several specified hours throughout the day and night. For the Desert Fathers of the fourth century, however, the process was simple. The desert hermit Saint Macarius, for example, explained his approach to prayer in fittingly spare language: "It is not necessary to use many words. Only stretch out your arms and say: Lord, have pity on me as you desire and as you well know how! And if the enemy presses you hard, say: Lord, come to my aid!" Saint Macarius kept his prayers stripped down to the basics, in harmony with the spareness of the desert landscapes he so freely roamed. Another form of prayer that he often practiced was called psalmody; it entailed merely the constant repetition of a small scriptural passage, the most popular of which was the prayer of the Publican: "Lord Jesus Christ, Son of God, have mercy on me a sinner!"

Each spiritual epoch has had its own methods of prayer. One will stress silence; another, study of the Scriptures. Meditation may be crucial for some, while for others the practice of poverty and evangelism will be considered the means to true prayer. The method that speaks most powerfully to many contemporary spiritual practitioners is called "the prayer of the heart," which simply entails finding the prayer that is most our own, the prayer that we feel comfortable with, the prayer that makes it possible for us to go deep into our own hearts until we arrive somewhere near the center of who we truly are. From this deep sense of heartfelt self-knowledge we are finally called to move beyond our self to God, to the deepest center of spiritual wholeness.

The prayer of the heart is based on a spiritual tradition called heschism, dating back to the fifth century, where it was practiced by the early saints in the monasteries on Mount Sinai. The word *heschia* is derived from the Greek for "response," so a Heschite was a person who responded to God's call in a state of perfect prayerfulness. In the desert tradition a heschite was a monk, an individual who lived alone, in silence, and in prayer. The twentieth-century Trappist monk Thomas Merton has done the most to revive the traditions of heschism today. "To invoke the name of Christ 'in one's heart,'" Merton once wrote, is "equivalent to calling upon Him with the deepest and most earnest intensity of faith, manifested by the concentration of one's entire being upon a prayer stripped of all non-essentials and reduced to nothing but the invocation of His name with a simple petition for help."

The consensus among the saints is that the vast majority of us are filled with hatred and therefore are unprepared for serious prayer. As Jesus said, "First go and make peace with your brother and only then come back and offer your gift" (Matthew 5:23–24). So the first great obstacle to prayer is hatred; the only cure for it, forgiveness. While this is relatively simple to understand, it is difficult to practice, for we all harbor anger over buried injustices done to us at one time or another. An unfair firing, the scorn of a friend, harm done to us by our parents—these sorts of things have a tendency to lodge deep within us, festering like sores upon our hearts until at last we find the courage to forgive. The saints believed that such angry, unforgiving thoughts raise a barrier between ourselves, our loved ones, and our God, reminding us that spiritual growth does not occur in a vacuum. The bonds we share with each other are as important as those we share with our God, so much so that we are enjoined by God to cleanse our bonds with our families, our former enemies, our bosses, and ourselves through the act of forgiveness.

Once the constrictions of anger are laid to rest, we can quiet our minds and begin to pray in a state of quiet solitude. Unfortunately, silence is a troubling concept for modern man. Think about it for a moment. Are there any true moments of silence in your life? Probably not. But to focus yourself in prayer, you must enter an oasis of stillness. As Saint Basil put it, "When the mind is no longer dissipated amidst external things, nor dispersed across the world through the senses, it returns to itself; and by means of

Thomas Merton, a monk who wrote many popular books on prayer and the nature of contemplative life.
(Thomas Merton Studies Center)

itself it ascends to the thought of God." The purpose of silence is to allow God the room to speak to us.

A popular technique used by the saints for quieting the mind is to concentrate on a single idea or vision, such as Love or God or the name of a favorite saint. By gathering our thoughts in this manner, internal chatter slips away and we are left with empty calm. The medieval saint Simeon the New Theologian described the process as follows:

> Sit down alone and in silence. Lower your head, shut your eyes, breathe out gently and imagine yourself looking into your own heart. Carry your mind, i.e. your thoughts, from your head to your heart. As you breathe out say: "Lord Jesus Christ, have mercy on me". Say it moving your lips gently, or say it in your mind. Try to put all thoughts aside. Be calm, be patient and repeat the process frequently.

Mother Teresa praying the rosary.
(AP Wide World Photos)

In looking beyond the confines of our mind, we soon discover a higher level of prayer that goes beyond the needs of our everyday life. Such an experience of true prayer, of God, liberates us from conventional thinking and opens the door to the realm of transcendental understanding and spiritual fulfillment. We need only look at the lives of the greatest saints in history, particularly the mystics, to know that it is well within our grasp to reach beyond our egos and out to God.

Prayer may seem a complicated subject at first, but it is really nothing more than the practice of opening our hearts to the Divine mystery—and allowing that mystery to infuse us with love. As Saint Teresa of Ávila reminds us, "Prayer is an exercise of love, and it would be incorrect to think that if there is no time for solitude there is no prayer at all." Prayer must have a central place in the life of any spiritually minded layperson, and regardless of the setting, prayer can be offered up by anyone at any time and in any way, provided it is offered with sincerity and love. We needn't be a desert hermit or a cloistered monastic to pray with sincerity, intensity,

and effectiveness. All we must do is put aside our pride and our anger and look to the heavens with humility, awe, and hope. As Mother Teresa of Calcutta says, "Love to pray—feel often during the day the need for prayer, and take trouble to pray. Prayer enlarges the heart until it is capable of containing God's gift of himself. Ask and seek, and your heart will grow big enough to receive him and keep him as your own."

While it is unpopular today in some circles to proclaim so boldly a faith in God, His saints and prayer, what better way is there to live our lives than by accepting the truth that we are all dependent upon God and connected together through His love, man to woman, mother to son, friend to enemy, human to saint? We need only open our hearts to this joyous spiritual connection to feel these ties and receive the graces extended to us through the communion of saints.

2

EVERYDAY

MIRACLES

*True Stories of Prayer
in Action*

*I*t is said that Saint Gothard hung his cloak from a sunbeam when he could not find a proper hook. And that Saint Sabrinus understood the language of birds and could be found preaching to them note by note. Saint Kenneth, while on a mission to Scotland, made the sign of the cross as an attacker threatened to pierce him with a sword and his assailant's hand was paralyzed. Saint Rita of Cascia was fed by bees as a child, while the Irish saint Bridget could request the trees to bear fruit for her, ovens to yield baked bread, and hens to lay eggs.

Are these miracles, or are they just the poetry of admiring biographers? It is hard for me to say. I suppose each of us must decide for ourselves what is miraculous and what is merely coincidence. An eminent biologist once told my husband that miracles, like the very concept of God, are nothing more than childish fictions created by people who are unhappy with their lives. This man of reason said that there is "nothing out there but science." Émile Zola, a devout atheist, spent much of his life seeking to disprove the existence of miracles, summarizing his view with the following simple words: "Even if I saw a miracle, I couldn't believe it." We've all met such people; they are full of pride and surety, convinced the scientific method can

explain away just about any "miraculous" event. Their lives are guided almost exclusively by reason, not by faith. They cannot understand miracles because they cannot fathom faith. And yet, as Louis Pasteur insightfully declared, "a little science estranges men from God, much science leads them back to Him." The greatest scientist of our century, Albert Einstein, was a humble, spiritual man who once wrote that "cosmic religious feeling is the strongest and noblest motive of scientific research."

Miracles, I believe, not only regularly occur but have a powerful purpose. They appear in our world to remind us of the presence of the Divine and our undeniable connectedness through His love with all of Creation. Since each of us, every day of our lives, is steeped in some particle of grace, some spark of the Divine, our very lives are miracles. Forget this, and it is impossible to be grateful for life; forget gratefulness, and it is impossible to be joyously responsive to creation; forget joyfulness, and it is difficult to love, hard to honor God, and nearly impossible to sustain faith.

Saint Rita of Cascia, who was admitted to the Augustinian convent at Cascia after the death of her husband, is the advocate of difficult causes. In New Mexico she is often invoked to restrain roving husbands.
(Denver Art Museum)

Perhaps the greatest lesson the saints have to teach us today is that a miracle is truly the very act of keeping faith whole, even when our prayers go unanswered. For without faith miracles are empty events. Without faith, we are blind to the everyday miracle of life itself. "All our life is a miracle," wrote Ralph Waldo Emerson. "Ourselves are the greatest wonder of all. I can believe a miracle because I can raise my own arm. I can believe a miracle because I can remember. I can believe it because I can speak and be understood by you. I can believe in a manifestation of power beyond my own, because I am such a manifestation. There is not a minute in the twenty-four hours that is not filled with miracles." Not all of us are gifted with the insight and faith of an Emerson. If we are not careful, miracles can and often do slip past us.

The main message of the saints' lives is how miraculously full our lives can be if we live imitating the generous heart of God. Miracles do exist, and I agree with Emerson that the greatest miracle of all is our ability to keep discovering them in our everyday lives. The pleasure I draw from a rich western sunset is a miracle—the miracle called beauty. The pleasure I take from sipping a fine glass of wine is a miracle—the miracle called taste. And the joy my family brings me is surely the greatest miracle of all—the miracle of love.

While many of the stories of saints' lives are filled with tales of miracles performed both during their lives and after their deaths, their greatest miracles were their unshakable faith in God and in the primacy of love. Their lives give eloquent testimony to their constant belief in the power of love— their love of God and God's love for them, through which all things can be accomplished.

The saints' lifelong devotion to the service of God is a miracle in itself, and a reminder to us today to see faith as the most miraculous gift of all. James D. Steffes, the pastor of Our Lady of Guadalupe Church, located in one of the poorest sections of Houston, understands this miracle of faith. The church's school, which for eighty years has educated the poorest of the poor, has an annual budget of $450,000, but must struggle yearly to raise that amount. Not long ago, Father Steffes feared for the school's survival as bills mounted and the bank account was draining. It was then that he began to pray to Our Lady of Guadalupe to help him keep the school in operation. And his prayers were answered. Here is the story he told me:

"One morning at five o'clock I was awakened by the ring of my doorbell. I stuck my head out the second-story window and asked who it was. A little old man said he had something important to talk with me about. So I put on my bathrobe, went downstairs, and let him into the parlor to listen to him.

"He told me a story of how he had been digging a hole in his back yard to bury a pile of bricks that were unsightly. Just as he was about to finish the hole, his shovel struck something that was hard and made a tinny sound. He dug out an old metal box. Opening it, he found lots of hundred-

According to legend, Our Lady of Guadalupe appeared to a man named Juan Diego, whom she twice sent to visit the Bishop of Mexico City to request that a church be built in her honor. These pleas met with rejection. On the third day Juan Diego did not visit the bishop because he had to care for a sick uncle. On the fourth day, Our Lady of Guadalupe appeared again, providing Juan Diego with miraculous roses, putting her image on his tilma and curing his uncle. These miraculous events identified Our Lady of Guadalupe as the Virgin Mary.

(Gift of the Historical Society of New Mexico, the Museum of New Mexico, Museum of International Folk Art, Santa Fe. Photographer: Nancy Hunter Warren)

dollar bills. Some were so badly damaged that they had nearly rotted away entirely. He kept a few for himself and came to me with the rest, saying that he wanted to give it to Our Lady of Guadalupe. He didn't want other people to know about it, because if they did, he feared, people would hit him over the head to dig in his back yard to find more money.

"Well, we took the money to the Federal Reserve, and they verified that it was not from a bank robbery, so they sent us a check for $9,500 for the bills, including those that had almost rotted away.

"If Our Lady wants her school to keep going in the midst of the poverty of Houston's second ward for eighty years and running, she will help little old men find boxes of money in their back yard to give to her Church. So I stopped worrying a long time ago about those bills. She knows how to handle it."

Hundreds of people like Father Steffes have shared with me their stories of a favorite saint answering their prayers. Since I cannot reprint all of these wonderful stories, much as I would like to, I have selected a small number of them to share with you here. These stories fit nicely into four categories: Prayers for Guidance, Cures, Lost Causes, or Lost Objects.

PRAYERS FOR GUIDANCE

Life is often difficult. Few of us would deny that. We may have health problems, career problems, family problems, and emotional problems. Even when we do not face obvious, big problems, we always have the daily smaller problems. Every day, we make hundreds of decisions that dramatically affect our lives. The late Norman Cousins used to say that "Every decision we make has consequences," adding that "Wisdom is the anticipation of consequences." But how many of us can effectively anticipate the consequences of our decisions? Very few of us, which no doubt explains why so many of the stories people shared with me were associated with prayers for guidance in making important life decisions.

How do we know when our prayers for direction are being answered? When can we feel certain we are making the best choice? There is no easy answer to this, for while prayer may direct us in our thoughts and help us clarify them, each of us still must decide how to respond to the insights we draw from it. It may help you in responding to notice how you feel about the answers you get in prayer: Do you have a sense of calm or certainty, of being unafraid as you think over the answer you received? Or do you have a sense of turmoil, upheaval, and inner conflict? When I am calm and unafraid in the face of the answer prayer has given me, I view that as the right course to follow. When I feel turmoil or conflict, I continue to search for another answer. Even a difficult course of action or decision, if it's right, can give you a sense of peace and certitude.

Sometimes we just need a little extra help in doing what we know to be the right thing.

"Saint Francis of Assisi is my favorite saint," maintains Marty Wolf, of Denver. "When I worked in Mexico, I used to visit the prisoners at the jail to offer them whatever solace I could. But I was very often frightened because the prison was a wild place and anything could happen. I would always say a prayer to Saint Francis before I entered the prison doors. I asked that he walk alongside me so that I could minister to the men without fear. Whenever I did this, my visits were better, both for me and the men. I knew I did not walk alone."

At other times, we need help in solving major ethical dilemmas. One of my favorite stories of someone who faced the need to make a serious decision and prayed for saintly guidance is that of Professor John Ounan of Maryland, who shared with me the following story:

"Years ago, before I began teaching, I worked as a court stenographer. At the time a very prominent man was arrested for molesting people in

If God grants my desires, my heaven will be spent on earth until the end of time. Yes, I will spend my heaven doing good on earth.
—SAINT TERESA LISIEUX

men's rooms. It was decided behind closed doors that the case against him would be quietly dismissed—that is, the chief justice of the peace and the man's defense attorneys decided this. The district attorney, however, was not in on the deal. The hearing was set for an unusual time and place, and the district attorney was never informed. The chief justice was able to dismiss the case against the man without any argument from the DA. However, the DA caught wind of the news and quickly had the man rearrested.

"After the first hearing the chief justice took me aside and told me to produce a 'rough draft' of the hearing because he wanted to cover up his own coverup. Well, if you know anything about court reporting, you know that a rough draft is not something you do. Either you report the facts of the case verbatim, or you do nothing at all. I was faced with a real moral dilemma: Either I compromise my ethics by producing this so-called rough draft and face charges by the DA later, or I report the facts of the hearing as I was witness to and face losing my job.

"I went home that night and asked my wife what I should do. She said, 'What would Saint Thomas More do?' Saint Thomas is the patron saint of lawyers. So I went to a local chapel and prayed to him for guidance. It was as if he were beside me for the two and a half hours in which I prayed. At last, I knew what I had to do. It was as if he had spoken to me in the chapel.

"I returned to work the next morning and produced a verbatim transcript of the hearing. I was fired from my job the next day. But Saint Thomas's guidance had been to report the truth, to act ethically, and that is what I have tried to do ever since."

Moral dilemmas, of course, come in all shapes and sizes—no two are exactly alike. Father Bill Sanchez of Bernalillo, New Mexico, faced the difficult task of deciding whether to serve his young parishioners or honor his mother's birthday. He was certain he could not do both. Yet with the aid of the saints, he was happy to prove himself wrong. Here is his story:

"When I was a young man in my late teens, I was very involved with the Catholic youth ministry. One year I was working on a program we called the Search for Christian Maturity during a weekend retreat for youths between the ages of sixteen and twenty-two. But that weekend fell at the same time as my mother's birthday, an occasion I had always taken to buy her lovely roses. That year I had very little money and wanted to buy some rosaries to pass out to the kids during a talk I was giving on the power of prayer. But I couldn't buy both the rosaries and the roses. So I told my mother about my dilemma, and she, of course, said the rosaries were more important.

"A short while later, I was home working on my talk and praying for guidance from the saints when I came across a quote from the work of Saint Louis Grignion of Montfort. The line read, 'Each bead of the rosary is like a rose being offered to the Blessed Mother.' I had just finished writing down this line when my mother returned home from work. 'Where are the roses?' she asked. 'Where are you hiding them?' I was surprised and told her I hadn't gotten her any, and she finally believed me. But she told me that when she opened the door to her house, a powerful scent of roses had overwhelmed her. I told her what I had been writing, and of the quote I had just read, and we both understood that this was a special message of love from Saint Mary and Saint Louis."

PRAYERS FOR HEALING

Since most of us prize the gift of life and wish to live as fully and vigorously as we can, it did not surprise me that many of the true stories I collected were associated with intercessory healings of one sort or another. What did surprise me was that the great majority of the men and women I spoke with were absolutely convinced that the task of healing was as much their responsibility as it was God's or their doctors'. Put differently, they were

convinced that they needed to maintain a hopeful, positive attitude to aid them in the healing process. As such, most of the men and women I spoke with looked to their favorite saints not simply for a cure for their health problems (although that was the ultimate goal), but for the kind of faithfulness and positivity necessary to assist them in the healing process. One such person was Georgia Photopulos of Northbrook, Illinois, who told me the following story:

"We have a large incidence of cancer in my family, so I guess it came as no surprise that on my tenth wedding anniversary I received a diagnosis of breast cancer. It was ironic, too, because everything else had been going so well in our lives. My husband and I were in love—we always said we were the perfect couple—and we had wonderful children. My husband had just been made an ABC network correspondent, which he had long dreamed of, so all seemed so perfect. That was in 1968.

"After my first breast was removed, I was receiving therapeutic radiology at the local hospital where I happened to chat briefly with a man from our church who was there with his daughter. I later saw him in church, and he asked me then why I had been at the hospital. When I told him, he wept openly.

"The next week, he was waiting for us at the hospital and told me he had something for me. It was a relic of Saint Nectarius, the patron saint of cancer patients in the Greek Orthodox tradition. Saint Nectarius was a twentieth-century saint, and this man had actually known him back in Greece. He had great faith in his intercessory powers, so he urged me to pray to him for help.

"I kept the relic and prayed to Saint Nectarius for the strength to make it through. I asked only that I survive and that he give me the courage to cope with my cancer. I also promised to him that if I lived, I would help every sick and dying person that came my way for the rest of my life. Since then, while I have had many recurrences of cancer—including a bout with a benign brain tumor—I have survived. In fact, I feel healthier than a lot of well people today. But I have never forgotten my promise and have become deeply involved in creating an emotional support network for cancer patients. My work even led to an American Cancer Society grant to establish the nation's first prototype twenty-four-hour hotline for cancer patients. I have never stopped working for sick people, and today I train others to work on the cancer hotline. Through it all, Saint Nectarius stands beside me as my light and my guide."

One healing story that is particularly dramatic was the story of the late William T. McNabb, who went on a pilgrimage to Canada in 1935 to visit the shrine of Saint Anne de Beaupré. His story was told to me by his granddaughter, Connie St. Louis of Denver.

"My grandfather suffered from severe headaches for nearly all of his life, the cause of which was unknown. At one point he had even been out of work for two years because of the pain he suffered. Doctors offered him a last-ditch chance to overcome the headaches with an operation to clean out his sinuses, but at the time they did not know what the result would be and didn't offer him much hope.

"Instead of having the operation, my grandfather decided to go on a pilgrimage from his home in Minnesota to the Saint Anne de Beaupré shrine in Quebec to pray for help, strength, and spiritual guidance. He wanted to be cured, of course, but if not that, he prayed for the strength to cope. He traveled by train with many other pilgrims, and when they finally arrived, they joined the priest for mass. There were services first thing in the morning and then again at noon, and my grandfather attended both of them. On the second day, when the priest raised the Eucharist during the noon mass, my grandfather suddenly got very emotional. He didn't want anyone to see him cry, so he reached into his pocket for his handkerchief and placed it over his eyes. As he cried, he looked down at his handkerchief only to find it soaked with blood. The man seated next to him grew alarmed and gave my grandfather his handkerchief as well. But when my grandfather placed this one over his eyes and then took it down to look at it, there

wasn't a drop of blood on it. In that instant my grandfather's sinus pain left him completely—and never returned.

"Everyone gathered around my grandfather, praising the miracle that had just occurred. In fact, they encased his bloody handkerchief in a box outside the shrine as physical evidence of the miracle Saint Anne had worked there. My mother was born three weeks later. They named her Bridget Elaine Anne, after Saint Anne."

Susan Solano Lopez of Westminster, Colorado, credits her survival from the ravages of Crohn's disease to the intercession of Saint Mary. While Susan has never been fully cured of the disease, she credits Saint Mary for giving her the faith and strength necessary to cope with her painful condition. As she shared with me:

"I was admitted to the hospital in 1981 with Crohn's disease, a degenerative disease of the small intestine with no known cure. I checked into Saint Francis Hospital in Wichita that year after already having been hospitalized twice before with serious bouts of the illness. This time, the doctors felt sure there was a small obstruction in my intestine that was infected. I had a temperature of 106 degrees and an elevated white blood count and things were looking pretty dim.

"I remember that a nurse came into the room and handed me a scapula, saying that the Mother Superior of the hospital wanted me to have it. It had a picture of Saint Mary on it. I thanked her and put it on immediately and began to pray to the saint, and from that moment I began to feel better. When my husband came into the room I showed him the scapula and then bade him good-bye. He was leaving to pick up my mother, who was flying in from Colorado. As he left, I saw the hurt in his eyes. I instinctively held on to the scapula and began praying to Saint Mary.

"As I prayed I felt a lifting and snapping sensation. I can't explain it other than to say that when I was a kid I used to cut open baseballs and watch the rubber bands inside snap. That is how it was for me—a sudden snap. The next thing I knew, I was floating in the air above my bed. I

To me every hour of the light and dark is a miracle. Every cubic inch of space is a miracle.
—WALT WHITMAN

remember looking down and seeing my crumpled body on the bed below. Then I looked over at a painting on the wall that I had earlier admired. It showed a river flowing through a field. Yet when I gazed at it this time, unlike the times before, I saw a man in the picture whose face I could not fully make out. He was beckoning me to join him, and I felt powerfully that I wanted to enter that picture to be with him.

"At that moment, the pain was gone from my side, a pain that before had almost been crippling. Suddenly I felt very calm and was sure that I had been cured. The next thing I knew I was back in my body. So I stood up—heedless of the IVs in my arm—and headed for the door to my room. The nurse headed me off and demanded to know what I was doing. I told her I was going home, that I had been cured. She ushered me back to bed and only then did I notice that there was blood on the sheets from the IV I had pulled out.

"I started telling them that I was healed, but they didn't believe me, so they began talking to me as if I were drunk or an idiot or something. At that point my husband and mother came in and were visibly worried. When I saw the doubt in their faces, I instantly panicked and began to doubt what had happened to me. Yet I quickly regained faith in what had happened and calmed down.

"Tests later showed that the infection that had brought me to the hospital had indeed disappeared, but the Crohn's disease remained. But I was not deterred. I don't know why God left the disease, but I told my husband that God works in mysterious ways. I left the hospital a few days later, but my life was changed forever. I embarked on a spiritual search that led me to volunteer at my local school and join a prayer group and a Bible study class. My life grew richer by leaps and bounds.

"Finally, in 1983, I had surgery on my intestine to remove the disease. After the operation, the doctors told me that they were astonished that I had lived such a full life with an intestine that had basically been dead for two years. But I wasn't astonished. My prayers to Saint Mary were an-

Madonna and Child with Saint Anne, the mother of Mary. Her feast day is July 26.
(Denver Art Museum)

swered. She gave me the strength. I found a faith that has not left me in all these years.

"Since that time, the disease returned, although I have been in remission for a few years now. My life is still rich and I have never forgotten that moment in the hospital when I experienced such a powerful spiritual conversion. I was saved by faith, and that was my miracle."

As the mother of a cherished four-year-old boy, I was especially drawn to the story of Carol Orlowski, of Dearborn Heights, Michigan. Carol had taken her three-year-old daughter to the doctor, only to learn that her daughter had a case of nerve deafness that would progressively worsen until she lost her hearing altogether. Devastated with the doctor's pronouncement, Carol immediately began praying to Saint Anne seeking her intercession with God for a cure.

"On the weekend after the devastating diagnosis, we were in Ontario on vacation. As it turns out, they have a Saint Anne's church in the city, so we went there to attend Sunday mass. As I rose to accept the Eucharist, I felt this all-encompassing weakness overwhelm me, and in that moment I just knew that my daughter had been cured. I told my husband about what had happened to me, but he didn't know what to make of it.

"Two weeks later, we returned with our daughter to the same doctor, and he found no trace of the nerve deafness he had earlier diagnosed. He was at a loss to explain what had happened but was happy to pronounce our daughter fine. We have never had any problem with her hearing since. I firmly believe that it was through Saint Anne's intercession that my daughter was healed."

Retired Chicago firefighter Tom O'Connell found his miracle of faith through the intercession of Saint Patrick and Padre Pio. In 1971, with seven children to support, Tom's health deteriorated to the point that he could no longer continue his work on the fire department rescue squad. As he shared with me:

"Things went downhill pretty fast, and my doctor eventually diagnosed

my illness as a neuromuscular disorder for which there is no cure. I was in and out of the Mayo Clinic several times, and in the process of it all, I contracted diabetes from the medications I was on. I became so ill that I was finally confined to a wheelchair. By 1975, I had dropped to 112 pounds from my usual 175-pound weight.

"In a last-ditch effort, I checked into the hospital with the idea of taking an experimental drug. But before I could take the drug, they had to take a bone marrow sample to determine if I was suitable. Well, they stuck a needle in my spine to draw the sample, and just as they withdrew it I let out such a scream of pain that I'm sure they heard it in the elevator. But at that moment the room filled with a scent of incense. The whole time, I had been praying to Saint Patrick and to Padre Pio for their help with this disease.

"As it turned out, I was not a good match for the drug, so they sent me home with little hope. I was left with nothing but my prayers to Saint Patrick and Padre Pio. Six months later, I had gained sixty pounds and was well enough to return to the fire department. And things just keep improving. I went on to finish both my undergraduate and master's degrees. And I retired in full health from the fire department in 1985. For the past five years I have been the director of the Catholic League in Chicago. I believe quite strongly that it was Saint Patrick's and Padre Pio's intercession that cured me."

Padre Pio was an immensely popular Capuchin Franciscan priest who bore the stigmata for fifty years until his death in 1968. While not yet canonized, he is considered by many to be a saint. Prayer groups devoted to invoking his name for intercessions are worldwide.

(Giovanni Rotondo, Maryknoll Fathers)

LOST CAUSES

The patron saint of lost causes is Saint Jude, renowned worldwide for his intercession in a variety of desperate situations. Every day, newspapers the world over contain hundreds of prayers to this admired saint, even though very little is actually known about him. One of my favorite stories about Saint Jude's intercession was given to me by Grace Natale, a sixty-five-year-

old mother of four grown children who makes her home in the suburbs of Denver, Colorado. For the past forty years she has prayed to Saint Jude, and says, "He has never disappointed me." Here is her story:

"By the time I was thirty-six years old, my husband and I had already had three sons. But my husband wanted a daughter so very, very badly. I wanted to satisfy his dream, but my doctor told me my childbearing days were over and that I could not have another child. But I prayed anyway that I might become pregnant with a daughter to fulfill my husband's dream.

"One night I had a dream in which my deceased grandmother appeared to me. She said, 'I told you if you would pray to Saint Jude he would help you, didn't I?' I awoke from the dream confused, because I had been praying to Saint Jude all along. What I didn't know at the time was that I was already two months pregnant with my daughter. My grandmother had simply appeared to tell me that my dream had come true. Seven months later, our girl was born, and we named her Mary. Saint Jude has never let me down. For over forty years he has been a source of guidance and aid in my prayers."

Of course, not everyone prays to Saint Jude for seemingly hopeless causes. Richard Schuler of St. Paul, Minnesota, decided that Saint Jude was perhaps a bit too overworked to help him. As he told me with a laugh:

"I have this theory that you should only pray to saints who aren't very busy, so I pray to a host of early martyr saints listed in the Roman Canon, a very old prayer. All of these saints have churches named in their honor in Rome.

"A few years ago I very much wanted to win a Fulbright Scholarship, and these are not easy to get. It's a long shot, you know, but I prayed fervently to these early martyr saints seeking their intercession in this matter. If I won the scholarship, I vowed I would visit each of the churches in Rome named after these martyr saints and pray there. Well, I won my scholarship and later kept my vow to visit all of the churches. I have kept

these martyr saints in my prayers ever since and have always felt their presence in my life."

Surviving the front lines during World War II can be considered a modern miracle, and Ulberigo Teri, of Maryland, is living proof of the power of faith and prayer. He admitted to me that, during World War II, "I prayed to a saint every chance I got.

"Perhaps my story is not so unusual, because everyone in the foxholes was praying almost constantly during World War II. The chances of surviving were slim, and for me they were even slimmer, because I served as a machine gunner in the infantry in Italy from 1944 to 1945. I saw some heavy action, and people were falling all around me, but I never got so much as a scratch. That I credit to the intercession of Saint Anthony of Padua. You see, my mother, who came from the old country, had told me about this saint as a young boy and encouraged me to pray to him when I was in need. I heeded her advice during the war and still do today. I have a relic of Saint Anthony that I obtained many years later when I was visiting Europe, and I still use it often to reflect upon this great saint's life and deeds."

Saint Anthony of Padua, the patron saint of lost items, is usually depicted holding a book to indicate his great learning. In this Mexican retablo painted on wood, the Christ Child is sitting on a book, an allusion to the legend that when the saint spoke, even Christ was enthralled.

(Denver Art Museum)

LOST OBJECTS

All of us lose objects from time to time: keys, watches, important papers, wallets, purses . . . But the worst thing to lose is surely an object that means a great deal to us spiritually. Such prized possessions are charged with sacred energy, making it impossible to place a dollar value on them. One such object in our home is a ceramic Chinese dragon that was left to my son, Aaron, by my late brother Kenny. Somehow that dragon, given with such love to Aaron, enhances and invests Kenny's memory with special beauty. Understanding how spiritually charged such objects can be, I was especially drawn to the story of Deborah Howell, a Washington, D.C.,

based journalist who lost the wedding ring that had been given to her by her late husband. Hers is a story of beauty and humor:

"My first husband died in 1981 from leukemia, and I wore his wedding ring on a large chain around my neck for months. I just never took it off. At one point when I was working in St. Paul, Minnesota, several of my friends were going canoeing and asked me if I would like to go along. I said sure, but I didn't want to wear this big ring on a chain around my neck, fearing that I might lose it in the water. So instead of leaving the ring onshore, I stuck it in the small watch pocket of my jeans. Well, we had a great day on the river, but on the way home, I discovered that the ring was not there. I became hysterical.

"After I got home that night, I spoke over the phone with my mother-in-law. I told her how I'd lost the ring and that emotionally I felt just bereft. I told her that I was going to rent a metal detector and go back the next day to see if I could find it. But we had pulled the canoe out on a huge beach on a big river, with hundreds of people going in and out all day long. Everybody thought that I was kind of silly to think I could find my ring—they thought my case was hopeless. But my mother-in-law said, 'Oh, no, no. You don't even need a metal detector. What you really must do is pray to Saint Anthony of Padua, the patron saint of lost things.'

"I said, 'You're kidding!' But she insisted, 'No I'm not. This is really important. Pray to Saint Anthony tonight and I will too. And you must call Rose [my late husband's sister] so that she will pray to Saint Anthony as well.'

"I said okay, but I didn't pray with great conviction. You must understand that I had no history of praying to saints, and no real belief in the power of a saint's intercession. After all, I'm a Southern Baptist. So I went up to the launch site on the river with the metal detector, but I had very little luck. I sat down on the beach and burst into tears and, almost in an offhand way, said, 'Darn it, Saint Anthony, you've really let me down. I asked for your help. Where are you now when I need you?' At that moment,

I looked over my shoulder and saw the ring sitting right on top of the sand. Just like that. Boom. I was ecstatic.

"I went home and I told my mother-in-law that it worked. I just didn't tell her that I had cursed Saint Anthony! She said, 'Now you must go down to the French church in St. Paul where they have an altar to Saint Anthony and leave them a lot of money.' I asked, 'How much is a lot?' She said, 'Oh, twenty dollars will do just fine.' So I left the church a hundred dollar bill as a token of my thanks to Saint Anthony."

No one will ever be able to prove that these stories are miracles, but for those of us who pray, we really do not need proof. Proof may be necessary to make a believer out of a doubter, but it cannot fill us with faith. Faith emerges from a deeper place, the spiritual center of our hearts, and for the hundreds of men and women with whom I spoke, it is the only thing that matters. This was also so for their saints.

PART TWO

PATHS

OF SANCTITY

3

THE COURAGE
OF CONVICTION

———

The Martyr Saints

*E*ighteen miles north of Albuquerque lies the town of Bernalillo, New Mexico, home to some seven thousand people. Nestled in a quiet valley with the wide and muddy Rio Grande running just to the west and the sacred Sandia Mountain looming to the southeast, Bernalillo is a picture of understated beauty. The town's most enchanting section is called the Concinitas or "little kitchen" district. This is the oldest part of town, where traditional adobe-style homes were built in long, connecting rows. Here Vivian Perez lives with her daughter, Olivia, in the temporary home of a statue of the martyr Saint Lawrence, the adopted saint of Bernalillo's fifteen hundred or so Catholics.

Saint Lawrence's statue hasn't always been at Vivian's house, nor will it be there six months from now. She has simply promised the members of her church, Our Lady of Sorrows, that she will allow anyone who wishes to visit the statue to enter her home twenty-four hours a day for the one year she has been granted to keep it in her home. She has waited eight years for this honor, a custom that has been practiced in Bernalillo for more than three hundred years. As she told me, "I was thrilled to host the statue. I always dreamed to have him in my house. When the statue is here, I

feel a special presence, like he was a son that I had here. We are very poor people, and Saint Lawrence was a martyr for the poor. And people have come each day to visit and pray to the saint for some help in their lives."

Very little is actually known about Saint Lawrence, who died in 258, yet his story has remained one of the most powerful legends for the poorest members of the Church. What we do know is that he lived in Rome during the third century at the height of Christian persecutions. Legend has it that when Pope Sixtus II was being taken away for execution, Saint Lawrence, who was serving as his deacon, began to weep and asked the Pope where he was going. The Pope replied, "I do not leave you, my son. You shall follow me in three days."

During the three-day period that followed Pope Sixtus's martyrdom, Saint Lawrence went all over Rome seeking out the poor who were supported by the Church. On the third day he gathered together a great number of these poor people and invited the Roman prefect to come and see "the treasures of the Church." The prefect arrived, expecting to see mountains of silver and gold but instead found a huge assembly of miserably poor and suffering people. He turned to Saint Lawrence in anger and asked him, "Where is this treasure of which you speak?" Saint Lawrence replied, "What are you displeased at? These are the treasures of the Church." The prefect immediately prepared a hot gridiron for Saint Lawrence, stripped him naked, and slowly roasted him over the coals. After suffering for some time, Saint Lawrence is said to have turned to his executioner and said with a smile, "Let my body be turned; one side is broiled enough." He then prayed for the conversion of the city of Rome and died.

As Our Lady of Sorrows' Father Bill Sanchez explained to me, "The history of Bernalillo's tie to Saint Lawrence dates back to August 10, 1688, when the Spanish Conquistadors came to New Mexico and attacked the surrounding pueblos with great ferocity. But somehow the village of Bernalillo was spared on that day, which is also the feast day of Saint Lawrence.

Saint Lawrence was martyred for refusing to deliver the riches of the Church to the prefect of Rome. As punishment, he was roasted to death on a gridiron. He is often invoked as a protector against fire and poverty, and as a guardian of crops that are harvested in August—his feast day is August 10.
(Michael O'Shaughnessy)

*S*omeone who speaks in
defense of a person who
suffers injustice will find an
advocate in his Creator.
—SAINT ISAAC OF SYRIA

*L*ike anybody I would like
to live a long life. Longevity
has its place. But I am not
concerned about that now. I
just want to do God's will.
—MARTIN LUTHER
KING, JR.

Many people died in the neighboring pueblos, but Bernalillo was never attacked. The residents were poor people then, and they remain poor to this day, yet their devotion to Saint Lawrence has never diminished.

"Saint Lawrence was a champion of the poor in his own time, and the Catholics of Bernalillo are convinced that the saint watches over them with special care. This is why each year, on August 10, the entire town honors Saint Lawrence with a three-day festival of thanksgiving for his protection."

The highlight of the Saint Lawrence festival is the matachini—dancers who have promised the saint they will dance in the festival if they are granted answers to their prayers. They wear caps that cover their heads with pictures of Saint Lawrence emblazoned on the front. The caps are meant to cover their egos as an act of reverence for Saint Lawrence as they perform their marvelously intricate and structured dances that wind down the narrow streets of Bernalillo to Our Lady of Sorrows Church and then back to the home where the statue has been housed for the past year.

The courage Saint Lawrence exhibited in the face of death is remarkable. While many of us admire the stories of war heroes and the bravery they exhibit in the line of fire, I suspect that most of us would agree with Voltaire when he said, "I am very fond of truth, but not at all of martyrdom." Truth is one thing—death quite another. After all, how many of us would be willing to do what Saint Lawrence did? How strong is our faith?

As I reflect on the life of Saint Lawrence and the lives of the first martyr saints of the Church, I am slowly coming to believe we may value life and fear death too much. If the martyr saints teach us anything, it is that some things really are more valuable than life itself, the most important of which is our faith, our guiding sense of values, our commitment to justice, truth, love, and beauty. For without these things, what are we? What could life possibly mean without spiritual values to live by—and maybe even die for? This is a troubling concept for modern men and women, but it is true that the readiness to die courageously for the things we most prize not only enhances our lives but sometimes prolongs them. The saints' lives tell us that we can battle with dignity for the causes we believe in.

Given the crucifixion of Christ, it is not surprising that the first saints of the Church believed that death need not spell defeat. For these early saints, death was to be the supreme imitation of the martyrdom of Christ. While they did not wish to die, they were convinced they would be rewarded in heaven for their faith.

The martyr saints' attitudes may seem a bit strange, even bizarre to us today. Modern usage of the word *martyr* confirms this. "A martyr complex" suggests someone who goes out of their way to find pain, producing a wide array of unhealthy psychological side effects. But the early martyrs didn't go out of their way to find pain—pain found them. They were faced with a choice: Do I renounce my beliefs to avoid this pain? Or do I cling to my beliefs despite the fact that I know I will suffer as a result?

Most of us move through life promising ourselves that at one point or another we will finally get down to the business of deciding what we really believe in. Some of us even promise ourselves that we will write a "mission statement" to lay down the goals of our lives. But we procrastinate. I certainly do. After all, it is easier to rely on the counsel and advice of others; easier to avoid the personal responsibility of actually committing ourselves to living by a set of deeply held beliefs. Contained in a tiny verse of Saint Mark is the greatest question of spiritual life: "But what do you say?"

Saint Stephen, the first of the martyr saints to be tortured for refusing to renounce his faith, knew the answer to this question. So did Saint Lawrence and the hundreds of martyr saints who died in more than three hundred years of Roman persecution. These early martyrs defied Caesar after Caesar in order to stand witness to their faith. Their fearlessness and courage galvanized and intensified Christian resolve. With each and every act of courageous defiance, they encouraged their comrades. For every man

In an effort to induce her to deny her faith, St. Apollonia was ordered to have her teeth removed by a judge. After the operation was completed, she remained steadfast. The judge then threatened her with death by fire if she would not deny her faith. She then uttered a prayer and walked calmly into the flames. She is the patroness against toothaches.

(Spanish Colonial Art Society, Inc. Collection on loan to the Museum of New Mexico, Museum of International Folk Art, Santa Fe)

Archbishop Oscar Romero. He was gunned down as he said Mass in El Salvador in 1980. Many people believe a case should be made for his sainthood.

(Maryknoll Fathers)

and woman the Roman Empire tortured and executed, two more stepped forward, and when they were killed, four more proclaimed their willingness to die for their faith. Each death charged and sustained the hopes of the earliest members of the Church.

The reverence of these early martyrs actually led to the establishment of sainthood in the Catholic Church. By venerating these inspiring human examples of Christ-like courage, the early Christians found hope for the present and the future. By praying to the martyrs, they found a way to close the gap between themselves and God, earth and heaven, time and eternity.

We continue to honor the sacrifices of these first saints on June 30 each year, when their collective acts of heroism are remembered by members of the Catholic Church. But these early saints deserve more from us than a nod just once a year. Their legacy is vital to our conscious faith. By remembering the courage that drove their sacrifices, we prepare ourselves for our own sacrifices, however great or small.

One recent example of an individual whose faith was emboldened by the courage of the early martyrs was the late Archbishop Oscar Romero of El Salvador. In an interview with a Mexican newspaper in 1980, he spoke the following words: "Martyrdom is a grace of God that I do not believe I deserve. But if God accepts the sacrifice of my life, let my blood be a seed of freedom and the sign that hope will soon be a reality. Let my death, if it is accepted by God, be for the liberation of my people and as a witness of hope in the future."

Two weeks after the publication of this interview, Archbishop Romero was felled by a bullet shot to his chest while he was delivering a memorial mass in the chapel of the Carmelite sisters' cancer hospital in San Salvador. His killer has never been found and probably never will be. But that is unimportant. What is important is that Archbishop Romero had the courage of his convictions. He chose to imitate Christ's life on earth by speaking out against the persistent evils of social injustice, poverty, and human rights violations. Through his actions and the actions of those with the courage to follow in his footsteps, the first saints of the Church live on, not only in Bernalillo but throughout the world.

4

THE WAY
OF SILENCE

—◆—

The Desert Saints

s I rise at six forty-five to begin each day, I try to remind myself to be grateful for my life and all that I have. Gratitude is the essence and goal of spiritual life. Yet I often forget. In my rush to put the cereal on the table, the butter on the toast, the orange juice in the glasses, I forget about gratitude. In the rush to fill my son's lunchbox, to wrap the scarf around his neck, to get him out the door and off to school with his dad, I forget; I forget to see that each and every act of our lives can and should be an act of prayer, a recognition of the blessing that is life. In so many ways, I see now that the great lesson of the saints is that the less we take our lives for granted, the more we come to see them as an "unearned gift," which has come to serve as my definition of grace.

Living a spiritual life is really about "waking up" to this gift. It is about cutting through our own lazy indifference and general unconsciousness to celebrate the marvelous "freebies" of daily life. My husband often says that the greatest joy of his day is lollygagging in the playground at the preschool our little son attends. Watching those innocent children frolicking around, he often tells me, fills him with incredible joy. It seems to us now that where there is great joy, there is much God.

Given my belief in the human need for joy, I must admit that my first encounters with the stories of the early desert hermit saints troubled me. Most of these fourth- and fifth-century men and women had abandoned their families, friends, and possessions to roam the deserts of northern Egypt in search of perfect solitude. The official Roman persecutions of Christians had ended in the fourth century, and devout men and women recognized that martyrdom in the manner of the first saints was no longer possible. Instead, they developed a new path to sanctity, a new kind of martyrdom: a self-imposed martyrdom of the spirit.

What a joyless lot these desert hermits seemed. What could a contemporary woman such as myself possibly learn from a study of their lives and teachings? And what, I wondered, really compelled them to give up the blessing of family and friends for the uncertain promise of spiritual realization through prayer, fasting, and rigorous self-denial? These desert saints initially struck me as escapist malcontents, spiritual zealots with a penchant for suffering. Why was it necessary for them to leave the cities for the desert? Why did they have to live in solitude and poverty? And just how could men and women find spiritual joy amidst such extreme self-denial? As I later learned, the answer to these questions is that we can achieve the habit of true gratefulness, true prayerfulness, only when we find an oasis of solitude that enables us to connect with the deepest regions of our heart. Such an atmosphere makes it possible for us to curb our selfishness, anger, and greed so that we may reach out to God with listening, compassionate hearts. As I slowly came to see, such deep connections cannot be forged without the kind of courageous spiritual independence and commitment to prayerful simplicity that the desert saints exemplify so powerfully.

In a world full of sleepwalkers, it is risky to answer the call of the heart, to wake up to the recognition that life is a gift. Living in a state of gratitude requires a different way of living. We can no longer be as mean or as selfish as we were. We must grow beyond our smaller selves to become better people. It requires that we change, and change is scary for all of us. Often

Sarapion the Sindonite travelled once on a pilgrimage to Rome. Here he was told of a celebrated recluse, a woman who lived always in one small room, never going out. Sceptical about her way of life—for he himself was a great wanderer—Sarapion called on her and asked, "Why are you sitting here?" To which she replied, "I am not sitting; I am on a journey."
—THE DESERT FATHERS

Legend has it that Saint Jerome was befriended by a lion when he removed a thorn from its paw.
(National Gallery of Art, London)

it entails long periods of loneliness. Yet Judaism, Christianity, and Buddhism all urge us to move beyond our fears and limitations through courage and faith. Like Buddha, the classic Eastern paradigm of faith, Jesus asked us to leave behind the world of comfort, family, and culture to "go forth from your father's house and country and come into the land that I will show you." The call to spiritual life is a call to explore the uncharted seas of our heart—a call that cannot be answered without courageous spiritual independence.

Buddha
(*Tibet House*)

As the father of contemplative Christianity, the desert hermit Saint Anthony (A.D. 251–356) has come to epitomize the idea that only through courageous renunciation of the material world and intensive inner-exploration in solitude can we connect with our hearts to reach out to God. "Renunciation," he once said, "is the dissolution of the ties of this earthly and temporal life. Only when a man is free from all human care can he turn his soul to heavenly things." Yet that does not mean, as I once feared, that we must leave our families and friends behind to reach out to God. Rather, as the saints of the desert taught us, it is less important to leave the world than to leave behind our attachment to the things of this world. These attachments include our popularly accepted beliefs and prejudices that promote division instead of inclusion, hatred rather than love. As Henri Nouwen writes, "We are called to solitude where we can struggle against our anger and greed and let our new self be born. . . . It is in this solitude that we become compassionate people."

Saint Anthony left for the desert, then, not simply to escape the city and its strife but to cultivate his caring, contemplative self. He desired the death of his old self so that a new and more loving self could be born in its place. Only then, he believed, would he gain the purity of heart he craved. He desired a death to his old self so that a new and more loving self could be born in its place. He also believed that his meditations and prayers would serve to counteract the evil vibrations and negativity of the culture around him. As Father Thomas Keating, abbot of Saint Benedict's

Monastery in Snowmass, Colorado, explains in *The Search for Meaning,* "This remains a deeply held conviction of both Christian and Hindu monastics: that the accumulated energy and spiritual power that comes from prayer and the contemplative life has an influence in diminishing the forces of evil throughout the world. In other words, if one is away from the distractions of self-centered activity, one is better able to refine one's spirit and become a receptor of divine energy. One may then transmit this pure divine light back into the world."[1]

Given that Saint Anthony was born some seventeen hundred years ago, it is remarkable that we know so much about his life and teachings. We owe this almost entirely to the labors of Saint Athanasius, who painstakingly recorded his life and theology in his now-famous biography, *The Life of Anthony.* According to Saint Athanasius' account, Saint Anthony was born to Christian parents in a village south of Memphis in Upper Egypt around 251. Shortly before his twentieth birthday his parents died and left him with a considerable estate with which to care for himself and his younger sister. Some six months later, while he was attending a church service, he was moved by the words of Christ to the rich young man: "Go, sell what thou hast, and give it to the poor, and thou shalt have treasure in heaven." Believing these words had been spoken directly to him, Saint Anthony immediately went home and gave away his best land to his neighbors. He then sold the rest of his estate and gave the proceeds to the poor, keeping only what was necessary to sustain himself and his sister. Not long afterward, he placed his sister in a house of maidens, the first recorded mention of a convent in Christian history.

Inspired by the Gospel that "we must through much tribulation enter into the kingdom of God" (Acts 14:22), Saint Anthony immediately devoted himself to poverty and prayer. For the next several years he wandered the arid deserts of northern Egypt practicing his own strict version of Christian asceticism. His only food was a piece of bread, his only drink a glass of water. He never ate before sunset, and he sometimes fasted for days on

God is the friend of silence. We need to find God and He cannot be found in noise and restlessness. See how nature, the trees, the flowers, the grasses grow in perfect silence—see the stars, the moon and the sun, how they move in silence. The more we receive in silent prayer, the more we can give in our active life.
—MOTHER TERESA OF CALCUTTA

end. He slept on the bare floor or a small woven mat. He spent his day reciting the Psalms and other parts of the Scriptures. Contemplative prayer was an important part of Saint Anthony's routine, aided by the constant repetition of a lone scriptural phrase, the prayer of the Publican: "Lord Jesus Christ, Son of God, have mercy on me a sinner!"

Saint Anthony continued to move from one solitary place to another, deeper and deeper into the desert, until at last he crossed the eastern branch of the Nile. There, at the age of thirty-five, he settled in an old cell on Mount Kolzim, near the Red Sea. His reputation for purity and piety rapidly attracted scores of admirers, many of whom placed themselves in cells as near him as he permitted, awaiting those rare occasions on which "their father" would descend from his "inner mountain."

The men and women who left for the desert in the spirit of Saint Anthony came to be known as eremetics. Although the eremetical path was a new way of life for Saint Anthony and his followers, it was hardly novel to his Hindu and Buddhist contemporaries. Hindus had been practicing asceticism from the earliest days of recorded history. And some two hundred and fifty years before Saint Anthony's time, Gautama Buddha spent a number of years as a wandering ascetic in an effort to sever his attachments to a life of privilege and ease. Only after he became convinced that asceticism was just another form of self-gratification and egoism did he give up Hinduism to practice his own concept of the middle way—a path somewhere between asceticism and hedonism. India and China also had long histories of ascetic practice, so it's possible that Saint Anthony came into contact with men and women who had studied these ancient Eastern systems from Aśoka's missionaries, who were sent by the Indian ruler to the Near East as early as 300 B.C.

The great seers and visionaries of the world's religions have always fashioned their spiritual lives through solitude. However, when Saint Anthony lived, solitude was a far easier commodity to come by than it is today. He needed only to walk through the gates of his city to enter the

Egyptian deserts, and solitude would surround him. Today many of us, engaged as we are in hurried urban lives, find it necessary to take occasional spiritual retreats in an effort to reconnect with the contemplative sides of our personalities. Yet it is important to remember that it was not privacy or escape that Saint Anthony sought but the opportunity to connect with the deepest regions of his compassionate heart in an effort to transform himself into a better person. It was spiritual growth he was after, and he recognized that the key to success was his willingness to change, his willingness to let go of his possessive attitude, his selfishness, until a new and more generous soul might be born in its place. As Father Keating writes, "If you are willing to change, or willing to let God change you, the kingdom of God is close."

Because spiritual growth and conversion is essentially a solitary endeavor, a private affair between a person and their God, the desert saints praised the role of silence in spiritual practice. "I have often repented of having spoken, but never of having remained silent," said one Desert Father. Words are great tempters to most of us, but for the desert saints and ascetics, the ultimate goal was to withdraw from the petty discussions of this life in order to hear the prayer of their own heart.

Over the past few years, I have gradually come to understand the necessity of solitude, silence, and prayer, and Saint Anthony and his fellow hermits now make a great deal more sense to me. They strike me no longer as curious products of a bygone era but as timeless examples of men and women who had the courage to confront their flaws and the willingness to correct them. Obviously, most of us cannot do exactly what they did, nor would we wish to. Yet it seems to me that Saint Anthony and his saintly comrades should serve as a reminder to us that we must be ever vigilant in our determination to live the spiritual life that we have imagined, and to cast off, as Thomas Merton puts it, "the domination of alien compulsions, to find our true selves, to discover and develop our inalienable spiritual liberty and use it to build, on earth, the kingdom of heaven."

Saint Ambrose.
(The Bettmann Archive)

Saint Anthony and these early desert saints taught us of the lasting importance of solitude and prayer. For this alone we must thank them, but we must also thank them for reminding us of the ever-present need to head out into the uncharted territory of life with courage, faith, and hope. The spiritual journey is ever and always a journey into the unknown.

5

THE QUEST
FOR BALANCE

*Saint Benedict and
the Monastic Saints*

*M*any years ago, when I was a young newspaper journalist, I once half-jokingly told my husband that I was going to "take over the world." At the time I held a high position at a large metropolitan newspaper and was convinced that it wouldn't be long before I became the editor-in-chief of a major U.S. daily. So filled was I with lust for an influential career that I thought I wanted it to the exclusion of all else. But today that phrase—"take over the world"—is a bit of a family joke, because somewhere along the line I lost that lust for power. A recognition of the need for balance and moderation in my life replaced that lopsided yearning for professional achievement. Since that time I have been drawn, almost irresistibly, to the life and teachings of Saint Benedict of Nursia (480–554), the saint of moderation.

Perhaps no other saint has managed to live with such art and purpose as Saint Benedict. Today, some fourteen hundred years after his death, his life's work continues to offer many lessons for spiritual seekers, including the importance of a wise spiritual teacher, quiet humility, meaningful work, and ardent prayer. Yet of all these teachings, Saint Benedict's stress on the need for balance speaks most powerfully to me, since I am a working woman raising a child and paying bills,

Saint Benedict is depicted on the right, where he has learned by revelation that Saint Placidus has fallen in a river and is in danger of drowning. In this miraculous intervention, Benedict has sent Saint Maurus to help Placidus and empowered him to walk over the water as if he were walking on land, grabbing Placidus by his hair to pull him from the water.

(Lorenzo Monaco, National Gallery of Art, London)

and through it all finding a sense of spiritual purpose and fulfillment amid the endless stresses of contemporary urban life. As Father Robert of New Camaldola Monastery, in Big Sur, California, explained to me, "Saint Benedict recognized that our life journeys take a long time, and that if we can order them a bit, find a rhythm and a balance to our lives, we can glorify God for the long-term journey."

Finding balance is never an easy task, yet Saint Benedict insisted that it could be done, must be done, if we hope to achieve a sense of spiritual harmony in our lives. He cultivated a balance between the polarities of solitude and community, labor and leisure, and doubt and faith and taught that this would prove far more workable and fulfilling for spiritual seekers than the extreme solitude practiced by some of the desert saints. He took this lesson from the laws of Nature, teaching that just as night follows day and winter follows summer, there are natural counterparts in the life of devotion: time spent working in the fields might be followed by a quiet moment alone, for instance.

Saint Benedict's Rule, or code of practice for monastic life, revolutionized the life of early monastics due to its sympathetic understanding of the spiritual quest. "We hope," he wrote, "that we shall ordain nothing that is harsh or burdensome." Stressing the need for moderation in all things, the Rule was very obviously crafted as a reaction to the excesses of some of the desert saints. While Saint Anthony taught us of the need for spiritual independence, solitude, prayerfulness, and the importance of turning our hearts over to God, more than a few of his followers also taught us of the greatest danger of the solitary spiritual quest: self-absorption. As the wiser desert hermits soon learned, and as Saint Benedict also concluded, the vast majority of us is simply not disciplined enough to advance spiritually without guidance, sensible rules, and a supportive community of like-minded seekers.

Not unlike the Buddha, Saint Benedict became aware of the human tendency to turn the spiritual quest into a form of self-obsession—the exact opposite of the goal of religious life. Surely the most bizarre example of misguided spiritual self-obsession was practiced by the desert hermit Saint Simeon Stylites (390–459), who began his spiritual practice in the Syrian desert by living on top of a six-foot-high column. He soon grew ashamed of his lack of courage since the column was so short. He then built column after column, each one taller than the last, until he finally was perching day and night on a column sixty feet high. His disciples gave him food and water and removed his waste with ropes and buckets. Then simply living on top of the pillar was not enough, so he bound himself to it, securing ropes so tightly that they cut into his flesh. Maggots soon feasted on his open wounds, and it is said that when they fell down, he implored his followers to replace them so that they might eat what "God has given them."

I must admit that I cannot understand why Saint Simeon was canonized, but I do think he serves as an important reminder to us that there is great danger in taking ourselves, and our spiritual quest, too seriously. He also serves to remind us of the danger of what sociologist Robert Bellah calls the excessive "privatization of religion" that is so prevalent in our world today. Convinced that our institutions and churches have failed us, many people set off on their own to find the spiritual nourishment they crave. A few are fortunate enough to connect themselves with God through disciplined prayer and compassionate action, but many others become mired in themselves and their own needs, drifting further and further from true communion with God.

As Father Robert observes, "One of the revolutions of Saint Benedict was to moderate all this post-sitting with a gentle rule harboring no extremes. His Rule gives us boundaries and support and saves us from just improvising on our own and going obsessive." Moreover, Saint Benedict's Rule of monastic life played a powerful role in reforming Christianity and shaping the future of sainthood in the Church.

Saint Benedict stressed the importance of spiritual humility: "The eleventh degree of humility is that a monk, when he speaks, do so gently and without laughter, humbly and seriously, in few and sensible words, and without clamor. It is written: A wise man is known for the fewness of his words." The only thing Saint Benedict absolutely insisted upon in the novice monk was that "in very deed he seek God." To do so, the monk was asked to work daily, to give up all possessions, to pray regularly, and to be obedient.

Obedience was so important to Saint Benedict that he opened the Rule as follows, "Hear, O son, the precepts of the master; so that by the labor of obedience you may return to him, through the sloth of disobedience, you fell away." As contemporary monk Brother David Steindl-Rast writes, "Obedience in the Rule means following the orders of the abbot, which brings with it a kind of freedom. One is liberated from willfulness, for it entails the humbly responsive listening of a person who has given his life over to God." In other words, Saint Benedict saw obedience to the master

Contemplation is nothing but a secret, peaceful and loving infusion of God, which, if admitted, will set the soul on fire with the spirit of love.
—SAINT JOHN OF THE CROSS

as a means of avoiding spiritual pride, to which the desert hermits often fell prey and to which, unfortunately, we all fall prey.

In addition to obedience, work was a major requirement of the Rule. "They are truly monks when they live by the labor of their hands as the apostles and fathers did before them," Saint Benedict wrote. He asked his monks to engage in the form of work to which they were best suited, so long as they did so with moderation. There was to be none of the bitter zeal of the "post sitters" and self-mortifiers of the desert. No useful work that could be carried on within a monastery was scorned, including gardening, baking, carpentering, brewing, and road building. Manuscript copying also became a popular occupation for monks because it helped to preserve the earliest writings of the Church Fathers.

The true "work of God," however, was prayer. Prayer provided the basic framework for the Benedictine monk's day. At two in the morning in winter and at three in summer, the monks rose and began singing the matins—a simple prayer consisting of Psalms and lessons. Lauds were sung at first light and after that, on the first, sixth, and ninth hours, as well as an evening service of vespers. The day ended with a brief service of compline, sung at sundown. (In medieval times, darkness and light were divided into equal periods of twelve hours. Water clocks were widely used before the invention of mechanical clocks to get the monks out of bed on time.) Saint Benedict's Rule included strict instructions for the order of the psalmody so the entire psalter was recited by the week's end.

Saint Benedict's Rule proved so successful and so spiritually appealing that by the fourth century many women desired to emulate the monks. They took it upon themselves to practice the rule voluntarily, but it was not until A.D. 530, when Saint Benedict's twin sister Saint Scholastica established a monastery in Monte Cassino, Italy, that women found their place in the world of organized monasticism. Surely the most innovative of the many nuns who followed was Saint Clare, who came to Saint Francis in 1212 expressing a desire to found an organization for women much like

Be watchful of time and how you spend it. Nothing is more precious than time. In the twinkling of an eye heaven may be won or lost.
—THE CLOUD OF UNKNOWING

The friendship of Francis and Clare is wonderfully depicted in this icon. The way in which they were faithful to their vows and devoted to each other remains an example for those who wish to be loyal to their own path.
(Robert Lentz, courtesy Bridge Building Images, Burlington, VT. All Rights Reserved.)

the one he had established for men. Overlooking canonical regulations, Saint Francis immediately received her vows and commissioned her to organize the Poor Clares. Fortunately, Pope Innocent III forgave Saint Francis for this papal transgression and confirmed the commission in 1216. Saint Clare set to work gathering other pious women who would live with her in communal poverty. It wasn't long before she became as popular as Saint Francis. She died in 1253 and was canonized by Pope Alexander IV in 1255.

Due largely to the leadership of Saint Clare and Saint Scholastica, Europe would soon have as many nuns as monks. While many of them were drawn to interior contemplation, most were filled with a spirit of activism. They nursed the sick, made clothing for the poor, and distributed charity and food widely around their communities. And for many centuries these convents provided women with their only opportunity for higher education. As the historian Will Durant writes in *The Story of Civilization,* "If we look back upon the nineteen centuries of Christianity, with all their heroes, kings, and saints, we shall find it difficult to list many men who came so close to Christian perfection as the nuns. Their lives of quiet devotion and cheerful ministration have made many generations blessed."

One of the great lessons of monastic life for lay people in our time is its reverence for community and its sense of shared responsibility. At a time when so many of us are cut off from institutions and are suspicious of community involvement, the monastic saints remind us that one of the great blessings of life is to find a community of people who support one another in their common quest for meaning. One of the most overlooked benefits of finding such a supportive community is that through sharing the chores of life (from child care to meal preparation to supportive conversation), community members suddenly find themselves with more time in which to truly live, to truly celebrate the gift of life.

Brother Steindl-Rast, who resides at New Camaldola Monastery in California, likes to say that the goal of community, monastic or otherwise, is to create an environment in which leisure is not a privilege but a virtue. As he puts it, "The leisure of which we are speaking is not the privilege of those who have time, but the virtue of those who take time." Take time for what? Beyond simply taking the time to enjoy the gifts that life, nature, and family bestow upon us—smelling the roses or listening to the hum of the wind in the eaves of the roof—it also means living in such a way that our lives become a celebration of the present moment. The monastic saints teach us that all our life is a gift that needs to be celebrated joyously. "To rejoice is to give back to God," adds Father Robert. "Births, marriages, moments of silence, these are the little glimmers we have of what our whole life is called to be, the celebration that is meant to be. If we order and balance our lives, this sense of celebration can be found in the most ordinary of moments."

6

COMPASSION
IN ACTION

——◆——

The Missionary Saints

*S*even years ago, Edward Sellner was feeling a growing division within himself. A middle-aged man, he had spent the past five years of his life working for positive change as a professor of theology at the College of Saint Catherine in St. Paul, Minnesota. His hours were devoted to almost nonstop action and social service of one sort or another, yet he felt a growing compulsion to pull back from the daily demands of administration to devote more time to writing and contemplative reflection. What was he to do? How much time should he spend in compassionate social action, and how much in contemplation?

Professor Sellner wrestled with these questions for almost a year before he dreamed of Saint Cuthbert, a seventh-century Englishman who yearned for a contemplative life yet was constantly pulled from his hermitage by the Church to serve the needs of the poor and the ill on the northern island of Lindisfarne. In his dream, an ancient Celtic figure with wild scarlet hair and a green robe bade Professor Sellner to join him in a life of balanced service and contemplation, free from fear. Yet as Professor Sellner stared at the figure, he grew increasingly uncomfortable, so much so, in fact, that he reparted the hair of this visionary figure, took off his green robe, and redressed him in a coarse brown

CUTHBERT
OF LINDISFARNE

Saint Cuthbert was torn between a life of service and one of contemplation.
(Ave Maria Press; The Wisdom of the Celtic Saints, *Susan McLean-Keeney)*

tunic. "As I later realized," he told me, "it was clear that Saint Cuthbert was trying to tell me that I didn't have to give up compassionate action in the world to satisfy my yearning for a richer contemplative life. He had managed to blend a life of contemplation and prayer with great social service, and he was calling me to join him. I was simply afraid that I couldn't do it at that time in my life. How could I possibly find time for sustained contemplation as a teacher, writer, and administrator?"

Later that year Professor Sellner took a sabbatical in Lindisfarne, where "I felt the living presence of Saint Cuthbert, who struggled with the very same issues I was struggling with. You see, in 679 he moved to a bleak and desolate island in the Farne group to devote his life to prayer but was called out in 685 to serve as Bishop of Lindisfarne. For the remaining years of his life, he devoted himself to compassionate service. I figured that if Saint Cuthbert could manage to balance action with contemplation, so could I. So I went on to write that book I dreamed about, *Soul-making,* and

later returned to my college to serve as director of our master's of theology program. And it has worked."

What Professor Sellner came to understand through his gradual awakening at Lindisfarne was the truth expressed by so many saints: Action and contemplation must go hand in hand. Each must inform and balance out the excesses of the other. As Mother Teresa explains, "These two aspects of life, action and contemplation, instead of excluding each other, call for each other's help, implement and complete each other. Action, to be productive, has need of contemplation. The latter, when it gets to a certain degree of intensity, diffuses some of its excess on the first. By contemplation, the soul draws directly from the heart of God the graces which the active life must distribute."

Finding a good working balance between action and contemplation is a frequent theme in the lives of the saints. A handful of them somehow managed to blend the two almost effortlessly, among them Saint Francis of Assisi and Saint Catherine of Siena. But most saints were not so balanced.

Saint Catherine of Siena, known for her many visions and mystical insights, is seen here exorcising a woman.
(Denver Art Museum)

Some felt a much stronger call to contemplative prayer; Saint John of the Cross, Saint Anthony, and Saint Catherine Labouré, for example, were clearly among these. On the other hand, Saint Gregory, Saint Dominic, and Saint Frances Cabrini were more greatly devoted to compassionate service than contemplation.

None of the saints, however, was either purely contemplative or purely activist. The only real difference between the activist and contemplative saints was in emphasis, and their focus in their adult lives was generally influenced by their upbringing and God-given disposition. Saint Mechtilde of Hackenbone, for example, was shy and timid from earliest childhood. She entered a cloister school at the age of seven, and from that time onward led a life characterized by silent prayer and mystical visions, not by vigorous missionary work or social service. Reared in silence and disposed to silence, she became a saint of silence. Saint Francis of Assisi and Saint Ignatius of Loyola, on the other hand, both displayed aggressive, outgoing personalities from earliest youth. Their boyhoods were filled with athletic and promiscuous endeavors, and both had dreamed of becoming glorious knights. Reared in action and disposed toward action, they became saints of action, although each was converted to Christian life through prayer, contemplation, and periods of intense self-abnegation.

The contemplative saints brought to Christianity the emotional and intellectual wellsprings of a deep spirituality of the heart, without which religion is nothing more than the acting out of empty rituals or the recitation of dead beliefs. Without the saints of action, however, it is difficult to imagine how Christianity could have survived. From Saint Peter through Saint Boniface to the Maryknoll Sisters and Fathers of this decade, the missionaries and social-worker saints have spread the Gospel of love not only by teaching Christianity but by showing it in deed. They nursed the sick, aided the poor, comforted the mentally ill, and educated the ignorant, thus serving as living testaments to God's unwavering love for all of His children.

Saint Dominic, a contemplative who was devoted to compassionate service, was the founder of the Order of Preachers. He was born in 1170 in Castile.
(Giovanni Bellini, National Gallery of Art, London)

While reflecting on the lives of my favorite activist saints, from Saint Vincent de Paul to Mother Cabrini, I have tried to isolate the common themes that bind them. Why were they so successful in their efforts to produce positive change? And what lessons can we draw from their lives and apply to our own? After a few months of study and a bit of late-night scribbling, I was able to identify eight specific yet interconnected themes that unite the lives of these saints of compassionate service. In the following few pages I will discuss these themes in the hope that they may assist you in putting your own compassionate heart into action.

OUR ACTIONS MUST SUIT OUR CALLING

Buddhists often talk of "right livelihood" and "right action," of finding the path of service that is most appropriate for a given person's skills and worldly obligations. Similarly, the saints talk of right calling, or right devotion. Saint Francis de Sales had much to say on this subject, for he was convinced that "true devotion hinders no one. Rather, it perfects everything. Whenever it is out of keeping with any person's calling, it must be false." I take comfort in Saint Francis de Sales's wisdom because there are many of us who are unable to devote a great deal of time to social service or community outreach because of the chores of parenting or of caring for our elderly parents or other personal or professional obligations. Saint Francis de Sales was sensitive to the fact that each of us must serve in a way that is appropriate to our needs, talents, and worldly obligations. As he wrote, "It would not do for a bishop to adopt a Carthusian solitude, or the father of a family to refuse to save money like a Franciscan; for a workman to spend his whole time in church like a professional religious. . . . True devotion . . . hinders no duty or vocation, but adorns and beautifies them."

Saint Ignatius of Loyola, founder of the Jesuits, in a three-dimensional bulto carved by Mexican santero Jose Benito Ortega.
(Denver Art Museum)

COMPASSION BEGINS
IN YOUR OWN BACK YARD

In today's world, with its mounting social, political, and economic problems, from global hunger to the destruction of the environment, from "eth-
nic cleansing" to inner-city race riots, it is easy to become overwhelmed by
the enormity of it all; easy to step back from the world and simply say,
"But what can I possibly do?" I've moaned about this far more times than
I care to admit. After all, the problems of the world are far too great for
any single individual to solve. But it is clear that the activist saints never
cared much about transforming the entire world—only their little corner
of it.

If Mother Cabrini, Saint Ignatius of Loyola, or Saint Francis Xavier were
alive today and someone said to them, "But what can I possibly do?" I
suspect they would answer the question in much the same way Mother
Teresa of Calcutta recently did: "Being happy with [God] now means loving
as He loves, helping as He helps, giving as He gives, serving as He serves,
rescuing as He rescues. . . . Therefore, even if you write a letter for a blind
man or just go and sit and listen, or you take the mail for him, or you visit
somebody or bring somebody a flower . . . it is never too small, for this is
our love of Christ in action."

Like all the great activist saints, Mother Teresa has learned that compassionate action is not a complicated affair. It needn't begin with a grand
sense of mission. We do not have to attend a seminary to learn how to do
it. We do not have to become President of the United States, or a Supreme
Court justice, or a small-town mayor to effect positive change in the world.
As Brother Lawrence, who worked in the obscurity of a Carmelite monastery kitchen for thirty years during the fifteenth century, once wrote, "It
is not the greatness of the work which matters to God but the love with
which it is done."

So whether we help one or help one thousand makes little difference.

*Saint Francis Xavier was a
disciple of Saint Ignatius of
Loyola and an indefatigable
Jesuit missionary to the
East.*
(Maryknoll Fathers)

Compassionate action is not a numbers game but a matter of waking up to the cries for help in our own back yard. Boston social worker Steven Wickson explains in *The Search for Meaning:* "All that God asks of us is that we be loving to those people who come into our lives. It's very simple. So you can be doing anything. You can be a waiter. You can be cleaning toilets. You can be a university professor. It doesn't matter. Wherever you are, there will be people present in your life who need your love and compassion."

DO GOOD
TO YOUR ENEMIES

A persistent message in the Gospels is to love our enemies, yet it is obvious that few of us today really take this idea seriously. Do good to those who hate us? The idea is somehow antithetical to all that we know about the world of contemporary commerce, much less the next-door neighbor who would prefer that we trimmed our lawn more often—and enjoys reminding us. Yet the saints were committed to doing good to those who hated them. Saint Ignatius once walked a hundred miles out of his way in winter to nurse a man he heard had fallen sick—a man who, just a few weeks before, had stolen his small store of money. And there is the story of Saint Spiridion, who captured a gang of thieves who were attempting to carry off his sheep one night. Rather than punish them, he set them free and gave them a ram, "lest they should have been up all night for nothing."

SERVE GOD
AND SERVE YOURSELF

By serving others we are serving God, and by serving God we serve ourselves. We can never be certain that our actions will produce positive results, but in striving to perform them as an act of devotion to God, we make a positive outcome as certain as we can. Our actions then become a celebration of God rather than an attempt to gratify our own needs or desires. Through caring for God's Creation, we thank him not only for creating us but for loving us before we knew how to love Him. As Saint John of the Cross reminds us, "God is love. We are not the ones who loved God; God loved us first. Let us love, because God loved first." For the saints, in offering every action to God, our life becomes, in Origen's famous phrase, "one great unbroken prayer."

GIVE WITH JOY, GIVE WITH HEART

Saint Teresa of Ávila once said that "I have no defense against affection. I could be bribed with a sardine." There was nothing smug or false about her. She took her life seriously, but she also took it playfully and joyously. She reminds us all that the best way to give is to give with joy, to give with heart. She instinctively knew that giving to others is a blessing, not a burden, because it produces joy within us. As Mother Teresa of Calcutta says, "God loves a cheerful giver. He gives most who gives with joy." To show that we are grateful to God for bringing us into this world, we must accept and serve others with an open and joyous heart. As the Ibo tribe of Nigeria say: "It is the heart that gives; the fingers just let go."

Love seeks no cause beyond itself and no fruit; it is its own fruit, its own enjoyment. I love because I love; I love in order that I may love.
—SAINT BERNARD

FOCUS ON GOD, NOT RESULTS

We live in a results-oriented world. As one New York brokerage house trumpets, "We measure success one step at a time." The saints thought

differently. As far as they were concerned, so long as we serve God to the best of our abilities, the success or failure of our social-service projects is ultimately unimportant. The lesson in this is that God asks only that we do our best, not that we meet with success. As the Bhagavad Gita counsels Hindu servants, "Be not attached to the fruits of the action." Jesus speaks of success as being "in the world, but not of it." With such an attitude it is impossible to get depressed over failure or self-inflated with success.

God is infinite concern for every living thing.
—FATHER THOMAS KEATING

COPING WITH SUCCESS

Accepting failure with grace and equanimity is the sign of a healthy spiritual personality, a person who is focused on God rather than themselves. But coping with success takes an even stronger person because so few of us are able to keep it from "going to our heads" and to keep ourselves from losing touch with our hearts; often, our humility succumbs to the seduction of pride, and God takes a back seat.

I shall never forget an essay by Thomas Merton on the subject of education. In it, he described an exchange he had with a man who had approached him to produce a chapter on a book he was compiling on the secrets of success. As Merton recalled, he responded to the man with the following words: "If it so happened that I had once written a best-seller, this was a pure accident, due to inattention and naivete, and I would take very good care never to do the same again. If I had a message for my contemporaries, I said, it was surely this: Be anything you like, be madmen, drunks, and bastards of every shape and form, but at all costs avoid one thing: success." As he went on to write, "Life does not have to be regarded as a game in which scores are kept and somebody wins. If you are too intent on winning, you will never enjoy playing. If you are too obsessed with success, you will forget to live."

While I am not certain all the saints would agree with Merton, I am

confident the majority of them would agree with its spirit: Success is immensely dangerous to those who believe it is theirs. After all, spiritual life is not about worldly achievement but the generation of hope. The goal is to know, love and serve God.

THE JESUS IN EVERYONE

Paul Holderfield, who founded a church, kitchen, and homeless shelter on the poor north side of Little Rock, Arkansas, is a man who continues to walk in the shadow of the activist saints. Although he grew up terribly poor and was never formally educated, he manages to provide for hundreds of destitute people daily. Holderfield looks for Jesus in everyone's face, and finds him "nearly everyplace. . . . I can find him ever' day. I found him in McDonald's the other day, beggin' for food. I stumble over Jesus ever' day. He said, 'When you've done it unto the least, my friend, you've done it unto me.' See, we feed Jesus about a hundred and fifty times a day. We give Jesus clothes ever' day. He says, 'I'm naked,' and we clothe 'im. He says, 'I'm sick,' and we take care of 'im. So the only way we can serve Jesus is to serve people. It's just so simple, and yet we just stumble. We want to do something big, but the biggest thing I can do for him is to take care of his people."[1]

The path of compassionate service is just that simple.

7

DIVINE

ENCOUNTERS

———

The Mystic Saints

*D*r. Alfred Painter is a tall, white-haired, eighty-year-old philosopher and retired college professor who makes his home in St. George, Utah. He spends his days reading, writing and wandering the mountains of southwestern Utah, meditating on the beauty of what he calls his "great outdoor church." Although he suffered the loss of his first wife to Alzheimer's disease some fifteen years ago and more recently the death of one of his daughters, he maintains a strong faith in God and the unity of life, which he credits to a profound mystical experience as a youth. As he shared with me recently:

"When I was eighteen years old, I lived on Queen Anne Hill in Seattle. My favorite pastime was to climb to the park at the top of the hill to sit and watch the city below and the surrounding mountains to the west. One day at dusk, a particularly clear and unusually sunny day, I became entranced by the movement around me, and my mind began to tune in to the complex, integrated mass of movement of the humans below me, all interconnected in various ways. I became aware of lights turning off and on in the official buildings downtown as well as in the residential areas. I became aware of the red taillights on cars leaving the city as well as of the headlights of the cars coming

toward the city. Rapidly, I became aware of the many other forms of connectedness. In the distance there were planes coming and going at the international airport. In my mind's eye I saw people from all over the world arriving in Seattle—and leaving it—and I personally felt this massive interconnectedness of life. It occurred to me that the vast, sprawling city was really like a living organism, with the coming and going of the people flowing like blood in the vessels of the planet—and I was an integral part of it.

"The overpowering awareness of my inevitable involvement with this mass of constantly changing interconnected life temporarily dissolved my sense of separateness and aloneness and brought me in contact with the unitive nature of God and all of His creation. At that moment, the walls that separated me from the world dissolved and a great weight was lifted from my shoulders. Sensing God and the surge of His life in everything around me, I knew for the first time in my life that I belonged in the world and that everything was as it should be. From that day to this, I have never felt alone or left out at any time."

Dr. Painter's mystical moment unites him with the greatest saints and seers in the history of world religions. For what he experienced so directly on Queen Anne Hill in 1932 is really the ultimate goal of all the world's great faiths: a transforming communion with the Divine in which the self dissolves to become united with God and all of His creation. As the mystic Saint Catherine of Genoa put it, "My me is God, nor do I recognize any other me except my God Himself."

Unfortunately, many people today view mysticism as a cloudy, mist-shrouded subject best left to saints and other "religious fanatics." In popular culture the term *mysticism* is commonly associated with things that cannot be understood. To be "mystified" today is to admit that we are dumbfounded by something beyond our comprehension. And while most mystics would agree with Saint John of the Cross that God is "infinitely

When a man is purged of all attachments to things the judgment is left clear as the sky when the mists have disappeared. His joy is not dependent on the creatures, for while his heart is set on none of them he possesses them all.

—SAINT JOHN
OF THE CROSS

incomprehensible," they would all agree that mystical insights are open to everyone and are essential to apprehending the greatest truths of spiritual life. As contemporary Carmelite mystic Mother Tessa Bielecki explains in *The Search for Meaning,* "Now, after twenty years as a professional contemplative, I've been able to understand that the very heart and soul of Christianity, which has been very obscured, is mysticism. Everything revolves around the mystical heart. . . . The mystical experience of God, the immediate intuitive experience of God, is what the tradition is all about."

Our contemporary aversion to mysticism is terribly unfortunate because all of us, to one degree or another, are mystics. In fact, all of us are born mystics, for the capacity to experience wonder and a primal sense of connectedness with all of life is our birthright. If you have ever experienced a sense of limitless belonging, or moments of deep gratefulness, or times when you sensed that all was somehow right with the world, you have tasted the fruits of mystical insight. The only thing that distinguishes the mystic saints from the rest of us is that they took their mystical moments quite seriously. As Brother Steindl-Rast writes,

> The men and women we call mystics differ from the rest of us merely by giving these experiences the place they deserve in everyone's life. What counts is not the frequency or intensity of mystic experiences, but the influence we allow them to have on our life. By accepting our mystic moments with all they offer and demand, we become the mystics we are meant to be. After all, a mystic is not a special kind of human being, but every human being is a special kind of mystic.

The great mystic saints of the Church have all said that even if our days are filled with nonstop service to the poor, we cannot afford to deprive ourselves of a contemplative life. And a rich contemplative life almost invariably leads to mystical experiences. For the mystic saints, contemplative

prayer was the heart of spirituality, the wellspring from which they drew their understanding of God, strengthened their faith, and nurtured their moral life.

Mystic saints have appeared regularly throughout the history of the Church (Jesus himself was a mystic), but they flourished especially during the religious corruption of the late Middle Ages and the Renaissance. A popular fascination with the ecstasies of the mystical life arose at this time, which encouraged Christians to turn inward rather than outward for reform. Much as the early Christians had fled to the deserts in search of solitude when the moral decay of Rome became too much to bear, the mystics of the Middle Ages turned inward to the desert of the heart. In their view, prayer was the only path to reform.

From Saint Anthony and the Desert Fathers to nineteenth-century mystics such as Saint Catherine Labouré, the saints have stressed that mystical experiences are nothing more than the grace-given fruit of ardent prayer. As sixteenth-century Carmelite mystic Saint Teresa of Ávila wrote, "I cannot tell why the whole world does not labor to draw near to Thee. . . . Only this I will say: prayer is the door to those great graces which our Lord bestowed on me. If this door be shut, I do not see how He can bestow them." Saint Teresa waited nearly fifteen years for this "great grace" until she finally experienced the powerful transcendental union she longed for. "We cannot make the day break," she wrote, "nor can we stop night from coming on. This prayer is no work of ours: it is supernatural and utterly beyond our control . . . we can but receive this grace with thanksgiving." So mystical experiences, like most of the good things of spiritual life, are the product of grace.

The blessing of daily prayer is something all of us can rely upon, but for the mystic saints, the level of prayer and communion with God occasionally reached supranatural heights. It is the intensity of these "supranatural highs" that distinguishes mystical experiences from ordinary prayer. In ordinary prayer, for example, it is easy to stay fixed within the present

Teresa of Ávila was a great mystic of the sixteenth century and was the first woman to be named a Doctor of the Catholic Church. Her tambourine reminds us also of her joyful, playful spirit.
(Robert Lentz, courtesy of Bridge Building Images, Burlington, VT. All Rights Reserved.)

or stuck upon oneself, but in a true mystical union this is impossible. Mystical experiences always pull the mystic entirely out of time and into eternity, out of the self and into a state of union with God. In this state of "at-one-ment," the great mystics are able to fathom the indescribable depth of God's love, not only for themselves but for all of His creation.

I once heard it said that "mystical experiences are to religion what basic research is to science." Mysticism is the well from which all great theology springs. The mystic penetrates the mysteries of spiritual life and returns to share with us his or her insights into the nature of Divine light. Perhaps not surprisingly, the mystics of the world's religions universally report quite similar experiences and insights, among them:

• A sense of oneness and unity with all of Creation. As the Roman mystic Plotinus put it, "In this seeing, we neither hold an object nor trace distinction; there is no two. The man is changed, no longer himself nor self-belonging; he is merged with the supreme, sunken into it, one with it." Or as the great Muslim mystic Al-Ghazali put it, "No higher ascent for the soul is possible, for there is no height beyond the highest and no multiplicity in the face of the Unity."

• A loss of self. As Meister Eckhart wrote, "I say that if the soul is to know God, it must forget itself . . . for as long as it is self-aware and self-conscious, it will not see or be conscious of God."

• An experience of light, love and joy, such as Saint Augustine experienced: "I entered and beheld with the eye of my soul . . . above my mind, light unchangeable. . . . He that knows the truth, knows what that light is; and he that knows it, knows eternity. Love knoweth it. O truth who art Eternity! And love who art Truth! And eternity who art Love!" The great Indian philosopher Shankara describes it this way: "I have risen above my ignorance and my knowledge of this seeming universe. What is this joy I feel? Who shall measure it? I know nothing but joy, limitless, unbounded."

• A belief that mystic truths are beyond reason and impossible to communicate with words. "Above my mind," as Saint Augustine put it; or "Above all natural understanding," as Saint John of the Cross wrote.

In the Middle Ages, the complete merging of the self with God described by the mystics came to be viewed by Christians as a sort of wedding with the Divine. Later, in the Carmelite tradition of Saint Teresa of Ávila and Saint Teresa of Lisieux, this Divine marriage was called bridal mysticism. As Mother Tessa explains, "through our mysticism we celebrate our oneness with Christ, with God, which means we are actually wedded to all of creation. All of creation becomes spouse. All of creation becomes bride or bridegroom. The universe is your body. . . . We know God as spouse or bridegroom, the way a friend would know a friend, the way a lover knows a lover, the way a bridegroom knows the bride." So the mystic becomes rooted in God's love instead of self-love, selfless in the true sense of the word.

Insofar as all the mystic saints came to possess the same unitive knowledge of God and His Creation, they are all very much alike. Yet each of them responded to the challenges of life quite differently. Saint Catherine Labouré's mystical insights inspired her to work against poverty and to bring about Church reform, while Saint Teresa of Ávila's visions called her to found religious communities where women and men could enjoy the sheer pleasure of God's company. Saint John of the Cross, on the other hand, used each of his mystical experiences to build upon the next and then to write about them so lovingly that he became a spiritual guide for generations.

The mystic saints insisted the insights gained from their encounters with the Divine were far more important than the encounters themselves. After all, deep mystical experiences come infrequently and last for relatively short periods of time. The question is, how do we behave during the rest of our lives? After we come down from our spiritual high, how do we fill

Saint John of the Cross, patron saint of poets, authored some of the most lovely mystical writings ever produced, among them **Love's Living Flame,** *and* **The Dark Night of the Soul.**

(Robert Lentz, courtesy of Bridge Building Images, Burlington, VT. All Rights Reserved.)

Saint Gertrude the Great is the patroness of devotion to the heart of Jesus. She was particularly popular in Europe from the Middle Ages until the seventeenth century. A German mystic, Saint Gertrude rejected the opportunity to pursue secular studies to devote herself entirely to contemplative life. Her writings would later have an influence on Saint Teresa of Ávila.

(José Aragon Private Collection)

the hours of our day? For those who take the spiritual journey seriously, then, unitive mystical experiences are hardly the end of the line—if anything, they are just the beginning. What is most important is finding a way to incorporate the abiding sense of union with God in all of our lives, and that entails tremendous responsibility.

Denver poet and social worker Doug Anderson, who has had numerous mystical experiences, has used his insights to inform his life of community service. He has visited prisoners, arranged community youth poetry readings, and staged numerous performances for senior groups. "Serving God is really quite simple," he said. "It depends on our willingness to overcome whatever it is in ourselves that we see separating us from other people. And those are intensely practical, daily, simple things. My first insights into this simple truth came to me when I went from Mexico to India as a deck boy on a Norwegian tanker in my mid-twenties.

"I'd be out on the prow of the ship every evening at sunset. The light show was literally three hundred and sixty degrees all around you and a hundred eighty degrees over you. Just all the way around for an hour and a half. And after sunset there's that wonderful time for which I have no better word than the old Latin *crepusculum*. It's a transcendent third reality between light and night. During this time, I'd be out on the prow of the ship for an hour or two in a state of rapture. At times I lost any sense of which way was up or down, which was sea, which was sky. And just as when I'm inspired as a writer, I lost all sense of self-consciousness and felt at-one-ment with creation. Therefore, in one of my poems, I've said quite clearly to the Divine Beloved, 'I don't need to believe in you. It's not a matter of belief. I know you. Help me. Help me to know, to love, and to serve you as best I can.' "

In much the same way, Saint Teresa of Ávila's mystical experiences convinced her that the ultimate goal of spiritual life was to give of herself to others by becoming selfless in every circumstance. Because of her mystical experiences she was made aware of the Divine nature in herself and in all other beings. That awareness taught her that even the most mundane and seemingly insignificant events must be met without malice, selfishness or greed, but consistently with love, compassion, joy, and a great sense of humor. As Father Thomas Keating so eloquently writes, "The graced energy received [by the mystic] from God, like an ever-flowing stream, is shared with those with whom they live and far beyond. Through them, God is pouring the divine light, life, and love into the human family."

PART THREE

—

LESSONS

OF THE SAINTS

INTRODUCTION

With more than four thousand saints officially recognized by the Church, it would take a lifetime of devoted study before anyone could truly call themselves an expert on the saints. The great eighteenth-century saint-watcher Alban Butler certainly knew this. He devoted four large volumes to his now famous but highly condensed study *The Lives of the Saints*, yet even he was still unable to acquaint himself with every saint. The task was just too great.

Faced with the problem of deciding which saints I should feature in this book, I sent letters to a variety of prominent scholars of Church history, among them a noted feminist theologian and a well-known Notre Dame professor. Along with the letter I enclosed a tentative outline for this book and a preliminary list of the saints I planned to profile. I asked these men and women to criticize my list and to offer suggestions for improving the book. The responses I received were wide-ranging. One respondent said that it was imperative I include more saints from South America; another insisted I include more women; two others encouraged me to seek out a few of the more exotic saints about whom little—if anything—had ever been written. Within a short time it became clear to me that I would never be able to satisfy everyone, least of all the scholars, so I decided to give up trying. What I did instead was turn to the saints who speak to me most powerfully, whose lives and deeds captivate my heart and imagination because they illuminate some significant aspect of spiritual life.

In the following pages you will see that the saints I admire come from

many different periods in history and represent a broad spectrum of approaches to sanctity. I chose to include a profile of Maximilian Kolbe, the martyr of Auschwitz, because he was one of the most extraordinarily compassionate and courageous souls in history. I chose to profile Joan of Arc because she, too, evinced enormous courage, although hers struck me as a far more reckless and self-centered sort of courage than Saint Kolbe's. Saint Jerome made it into these pages not because I adore him, but because I don't. His life was marred by an angry, confrontational style, yet I learned as much from him as I have from any other saint.

Despite the fact that contemporary feminist theologians frequently disparage Saint Augustine for his undeniable chauvinism, I couldn't bear to leave him out. I found little difficulty forgiving him for his antiquated views of women because his theological insights have enriched me immeasurably. Mother Elizabeth Seton is profiled here because she taught me much about the nature of tragedy and how to cope with it through faithfulness and steadfastness. And Saint Francis—that most popular of saints about whom so much is already known—why did I include him? I did so simply because he had been my brother Kenny's favorite saint, and because a statue of the gentle friar rests peacefully atop a hill overlooking Kenny's grave.

Mother Frances Cabrini is featured in these pages because she charmed me with her simple, down-to-earth humor and get-to-the-task, make-no-bones-about-it spirituality. To her, there was nothing complicated about the path of compassionate service. She never lost her will and therefore always found "the way." I chose to profile Saint Patrick because most of us are familiar only with his legend, which is far less interesting than his real life. Saint Teresa of Ávila and Saint John of the Cross are profiled together here because they were not only partners in crime but partners in spirit. Saint Teresa pulled Saint John into the affairs of man, while he pulled her closer to the affairs of the heart. Together they did more to improve the quality of Christian mystical life than any two saints in history.

The beautiful thing about the saints is that they give us not only philosophy but biography, for they represent living examples of spiritual truth. The founders of the early Church, and Jesus in particular, must be credited for this emphasis on "living story," for they instinctively recognized that all of us learn better from incarnations, from people who serve as models, than we do from lofty abstractions or set-in-stone dogmas. In the Buddhist tradition a similar wisdom prevails, for the faithful are encouraged to study the lives of the great bodhisattvas, the compassionate ones who could have chosen Nirvana but chose instead to remain on earth to assist the suffering. Likewise, in the Catholic tradition, we have the saints—men and women whose lives serve as living embodiments of Christian principles in action. They endure not only because they lived with great spiritual purpose but because they call each of us to do the same today.

Bodhisattva in the meditation posture.
(Robert Newman. Courtesy, British Museum)

8

THE APOSTLE
OF AUSCHWITZ

Saint Maximilian Kolbe

*I*n August 1941, Saint Maximilian Kolbe's fate was sealed. A prisoner had escaped from cellblock fourteen in Auschwitz, and SS Kommandant Rudolf Höss ordered Deputy Commander Fritsch to punish the remaining prisoners for the affront to Nazi rule. Fritsch assembled the six hundred men from cellblock fourteen in the prison yard and said, "In reprisal for your comrade's escape, ten of you will die by starvation. Next time, it will be twenty."

The selection began immediately. Francis Mleczko, a survivor, recounted the scene at Saint Kolbe's beatification hearing: "I was in about the fifth or sixth row back and the fifth or sixth man from the end Fritsch started at. As he came closer and closer, my heart was pounding. Let him pass, let him pass me, oh pass, pass, I was praying. But no. He stopped directly before me. . . . Then, in Polish, Fritsch orders, 'Open your mouth.' I open. He looks. He walks on. I breathe again."[1]

Deputy Commander Fritsch moved down the line, capriciously selecting the innocent who would die by starvation. When Fritsch had finished with his selection, one of the condemned men began to sob, "My wife and my children!" It was Francis Gajowniczek, a forty-year-old Polish army sergeant.

Father Maximilian Kolbe was a prisoner at Auschwitz, the infamous Nazi death camp in Poland in World War II. Here he requests of Deputy Commandant Fritsch that he be allowed to take the place of one of the ten prisoners condemned to die in reprisal for an escapee who had not been found. The scene has been immortalized by Polish artist Professor Miecislaus Koscielniak, a fellow prisoner at Auschwitz.
(Franciscan Friars of Marytown)

As Gajowniczek continued to sob, a prisoner from the back of the pack pushed his way forward. Alarmed, the Nazi guards ordered the prisoner to halt or be shot. The bold prisoner was Father Maximilian Kolbe. "Herr Kommandant, I wish to make a request, please," asked Kolbe.

"What do you want?" said Fritsch.

"I want to die in place of this prisoner," replied Kolbe, pointing at Gajowniczek. "I have no wife or children. Besides, I'm old and not good for anything. He's in better condition."

"Who are you?" Fritsch demanded.

"A Catholic priest," said Kolbe.

"Request granted," snapped Fritsch.

Maximilian Kolbe stepped forward, and Gajowniczek stepped back. The exchange had been made.

On August 14, 1941, after surviving two weeks in the starvation bunker, Saint Maximilian Kolbe was murdered by the Nazis with an injection of carbolic acid. The following morning his body was incinerated in the Auschwitz crematorium.

Word of Saint Kolbe's supreme heroism spread rapidly through the camp. Soon transferred prisoners carried the news to other camps. The effect of Kolbe's selfless heroism was summed up by Auschwitz survivor George Bilecki, who testified during Kolbe's beatification hearings in 1971:

"It was an enormous shock to the whole camp. We became aware that someone among us in this spiritual dark night of the soul was raising the standard of love on high. Someone unknown, like everyone else, tortured and bereft of name and social standing, went to a horrible death for the sake of someone not even related to him. Therefore it is not true, we cried, that humanity is cast down and trampled in the mud, overcome by oppressors, and overwhelmed by hopelessness. Thousands of prisoners were convinced the true world continued to exist and that our torturers would not be able to destroy it. More than one individual began to look within himself for this real world, found it, and shared it with his camp companion, strengthening both in this encounter with evil. To say that Father Kolbe died for us or for that person's family is too great a simplification. His death was the salvation of thousands. And on this, I would say, rests the greatness of that death. That's how we felt about it. And as long as we live, we who were at Auschwitz will bow our heads in memory of it, as at that time we bowed our heads before the bunker of death by starvation. That was a shock full of optimism, regenerating and giving strength; we were stunned by his act, which became for us a mighty explosion of light in the dark camp."

If you only knew how happy I am! My heart is full of that peace and joy which can be experienced even here on earth. Yes, in spite of the anxieties and worries of each day, at the bottom of my heart is always a peace and joy I can't describe.
—SAINT MAXIMILIAN KOLBE

Who was this saint of Auschwitz? This man who would die for an unknown friend? This man whom Pope John Paul II considers his spiritual hero?

By all accounts, Maximilian Kolbe was an unpretentious, warm-hearted, and immensely human person who once said he wanted nothing more from life than to "learn how to love without limits."

Born to a poor Polish family of piecework weavers in the town of Zduńska Wola in 1894, Kolbe was one of five children. In October 1912, by virtue of the great intellectual gifts he exhibited as a student at a Franciscan priory, he was sent to the Pontifical Gregorian University in Rome, where he studied for doctorates in both philosophy and sacred theology. His studies were delayed, however, when he contracted a severe case of tuberculosis. During the long months of his bed-ridden recovery, he solidified his desire to become an evangelist. And so, after earning his second doctorate in July 1919, he returned to Poland and immediately began publishing *The Knight of the Immaculata,* a free magazine dedicated to bringing news of the Catholic Church and its teachings to lay readers.

Maximilian Kolbe as a young seminarian.
(Franciscan Friars of Marytown)

The *Knight,* as it came to be called, was an instant success. So successful, in fact, that to handle the ever-increasing volume of work associated with its publication, Kolbe and his fellow Franciscans built a large friary and printing plant just west of Warsaw in 1927 on land that was donated to them by a local prince. He named the friary Niepokalanow, which means "the property of Mary."

Saint Kolbe had a lifelong devotion to Mary because she came to him in a vision as a little boy to promise him a life of purity and warn him of his future martyrdom. As his mother recalled after his death: "I have always known that [my son] was going to die a martyr because of an extraordinary event in his childhood. . . . One time I didn't like something about him, and I said to him, 'My little son, I don't know what's going to become of you!' After this I never thought about my remark, but I soon noticed that my child had changed so much that he was unrecognizable. We had a little

hidden altar [in the house] at which he was frequently hiding himself. In general his behavior seemed older than his years. He was always . . . serious, and praying with tears in his eyes. I got worried that perhaps he was ill, so I asked him, 'What's wrong with you?' I insisted, 'You have to tell Mama everything.'

"Trembling and with tears in his eyes, he told me, 'When you said to me, "What will become of you?" I prayed very hard to Our Lady to tell me what would become of me. And later in the church I prayed again. Then the Virgin Mother appeared to me holding in her hands two crowns, one white and one red. She looked at me with love, and she asked me if I would like to have them. The white meant that I would remain pure, and the red that I would be a martyr. I answered, yes, I wanted them. Then the Virgin looked at me tenderly and disappeared.' "

Father Maximilian Kolbe at his desk in Nagasaki, Japan, from which he directed the by then international Knights of the Immaculate and prepared classes as seminary professor.
(Franciscan Friars of Marytown)

So Saint Kolbe knew of his fate even as a little boy, although he never shared this story with anyone but his mother. But he had work to do before he left this world, so he threw himself into managing the daily operation of Niepokalanow. Within two years of its foundation, there were nearly 150 brothers working and worshiping at Niepokalanow. By 1938, it was the largest friary in the world, boasting eight hundred brothers and eleven publications. The *Knight* alone had a circulation of more than one million copies. As one of the brothers recalls: "The place was going almost twenty-four hours a day. . . . Father Kolbe was a very progressive man. He said, 'If Jesus or Saint Francis were alive now, they'd use modern technology to reach the people.' So before World War II, Niepokalanow had a radio station, was preparing for television, had the daily paper, and so on. He said, 'The more you know, the better you can serve God.' "

When the Nazis invaded Poland on September 1, 1939, Kolbe's publishing ventures began to crumble. Since Niepokalanow was in the direct flight path of German bombers, he asked many of his brothers to leave the friary for their safety. Father Kolbe remained at Niepokalanow to administer the opening of the friary to refugees. At times the friary took in as many as three thousand people a day. Father Kolbe ensured that they were fed, clothed, given medical care, and if necessary, spiritual counseling. It is said that he displayed an especially tender love for Jews and never turned a needy refugee away.

The Nazis halted the publications at Niepokalanow on February 17, 1941, and arrested Father Kolbe for treason. He was then taken to Pawiak prison. In May 1941 he was transferred to Auschwitz.

So it was that in August 1941, in keeping with the highest examples of Christian charity and courage, prisoner number 16,670 gave his life so that another might live. On November 9, 1982, Pope John Paul II declared Maximilian Kolbe a saint: "And so, in virtue of my apostolic authority I have decreed that Maximilian Maria Kolbe, who after his beatification was venerated as a confessor, shall henceforth be venerated also as a martyr."

Father Maximilian Kolbe hearing confessions at Auschwitz.

(Franciscan Friars of Marytown)

Sigmund Gorson, who entered Auschwitz at the age of thirteen, knew Maximilian Kolbe well in the camp. His memories of Saint Kolbe serve to remind us that wherever there is love, no matter how desperate the circumstances, light will continue to shine.

"I was always looking for some link to my murdered parents, trying to find a friend of my father's, a neighbor—someone in that mass of humanity who had known them so I would not feel so alone.

"And that is how Kolbe found me wandering around, so to speak, looking for someone to connect with. He was like an angel to me. Like a mother hen, he took me in his arms. He used to wipe away my tears. I believe in God more since that time. Because of the deaths of my parents I had been asking, Where is God? and had lost faith. Kolbe gave me that faith back."[2]

As I reflect on the many photographs I have seen of Saint Maximilian Kolbe, I am struck by how much his face and demeanor remind me of our greatest contemporary saint-to-be, Mother Teresa of Calcutta. They both share a quality the Psalms describe as "the beauty of holiness," a halolike quality of pervasive luminosity and brilliance. A calm, kindly, otherworldliness illuminates their faces, despite the fact that Saint Kolbe was just as practical and down-to-earth as Mother Teresa, just as fixated on serving others with all the tremendous heartfelt energy he possessed. Saint Kolbe also shared with Mother Teresa a love for Saint Francis and for laughter, even though each of them grounded their lives in the service of the suffering. Through all of the horrors of Auschwitz, Maximilian Kolbe held on to his essential humanity, just as Mother Teresa has held on to hers in the desperate poverty of India's slums. Through their caring sensitivity to lives of others, they each came to understand the great wisdom of Saint Paul: "Where the spirit of the Lord is, there is liberty."

A PRAYER
TO SAINT KOLBE

For Courage

Through your life and work you proved that nothing is more precious than our essential humanity. I pray that you will stand by me and give me the courage to act everyday with the sense of fairness, compassion, and respect for all living things that you exemplified. You have shown that great faith may call for noble and heroic action. If I am to be true to myself, Saint Kolbe, I pray that you will stand with me also in my most difficult hours. Be a reminder to me that I must have the courage of my convictions. Help me to imbue my every action with meaning and to have the courage to find the greater meaning and purpose to which I seek to dedicate my life.

The last photograph made of Saint Maximilian Kolbe, December 1940, probably for identification purposes under the Nazi occupation.
(Franciscan Friars of Marytown)

9

THE WILL
TO BELIEVE

Saint Joan of Arc

I've always respected the virtue of quiet reserve, but I much prefer audacity and persistence in my friends—and especially in my saints. Perhaps this explains why Joan of Arc, patron saint of France and martyr, has captivated me for more than twenty years, for she is one of the most courageous, tragic, and immensely human figures in the roster of saints. Outrageous and audacious from start to finish, her iron will has served as an inspiration to millions for hundreds of years. She was a pioneer for the causes of freedom, nationalism, and feminism and, as George Bernard Shaw once so humorously put it, "a pioneer of rational dressing for women."

While historians may disagree on some facts regarding Saint Joan's life, they all agree that she was born on the Feast of the Epiphany, January 6, 1412, and that the France of her youth was on the verge of collapse. The Hundred Years War between England and France had been under way for seventy-five years at the time of her birth, and French morale was deteriorating day by day as the English army racked up victory after victory. The war took a dramatic turn for the worse in Saint Joan's seventh year, 1419, when England's King Henry V overran Paris and forced French King Charles VI to renounce his throne and

disown his son the dauphin, Charles VII, who was holding out in the south of France.

Over the following six-year period the dauphin barely managed to survive. But by 1428, when the English army moved south to lay siege to the city of Orleans, the dauphin's forces were in such a state of disarray that they took no action to resist the English army. During this desperate time, in her sixteenth year, Saint Joan began to hear heavenly voices. At first she heard but a single voice, accompanied by a blaze of light: " . . . came this voice about noon, in the summertime, in my father's garden. . . . I heard the voice coming from the church . . . a great light." As time passed, she began to hear a variety of voices, most often "when the bells tolled, at the hour of nightsong, and in the morning." She was able to identify them as those of Saint Michael the archangel, Saint Catherine of Alexandria (one of the most popular saints of Joan's time who was said to have been tortured on a wheel), and Saint Margaret of Antioch, another legendary martyr. Initially, the voices spoke only of aiding God. But in May 1428, when Saint Joan reached sixteen, the voices told her to help the King of France reclaim his kingdom. "Go, daughter of God," Saint Michael said to her. "I will be helping you. Go! Go! Go!"

Despite the seeming futility of fulfilling Saint Michael's request, Saint Joan was determined to persuade the dauphin to wrest his rightful throne from the English. Her first step was to convince her cousin to take her to meet with Robert Baudricourt, the commander of the dauphin's army in the area of Vaucouleurs. Understandably, Baudricourt laughed at the sight of the young maid and rejected her request to be taken to see the deposed king.

Upon returning home, Saint Joan relayed Baudricourt's rejection to the saints, adding that she knew nothing about fighting and could not understand why they had chosen her for such an arduous mission. They replied simply, "It is God who commands it." Unwilling to turn her back on God's will, she returned to petition Baudricourt. Impressed with her tenacity and

compelled to believe her because her earlier prediction of a distant French army's defeat had proven true, Baudricourt consented to send her with an escort to see the dauphin in Chinon.

The dauphin greeted Saint Joan coldly. In fact, so skeptical was he of the young maid that he put her to a test. Before they met, he disguised himself as a courtly guest, and he put his royal robes on one of his courtiers. Yet when Joan entered the palace, she immediately identified Dauphin Charles, walking up to him and telling him of private thoughts that he had shared with no one but God. Impressed but still uncertain of her worthiness, the dauphin required her to submit to an examination by a panel of Church authorities at Poitiers. After weeks of interrogation, the panel concluded that Saint Joan had indeed been sent by God, and that Dauphin Charles should lend her assistance. When asked by the panel why she felt so sure of her mission, Saint Joan said, "I believed it was an angel speaking to me, and I had the will to believe."

The dauphin appointed Saint Joan supreme commander of the French army at the age of seventeen, and she instantly proved to be a skilled and tireless organizer and brilliant military tactician. Before her troops set out for the famous battle of Orleans on April 29, 1429, Saint Joan insisted they all attend confession. And when they began their march, she placed a group of chanting priests in the lead, while she herself followed close behind clad in white armor, with the words *Jesus Maria* inscribed on her chestplate.

Her decisive victory at Orleans was followed by a string of brilliant military victories, climaxing with the battle of Patay on June 18, 1429. That same year Charles was crowned king. But the tide turned against her on May 23, 1430, when she led a charge against the Burgundians, who had sided with the English. As the battle began to turn against her army, their escape was blocked, and Saint Joan was captured by the Burgundian John of Luxembourg. She remained in Luxembourg's prison until November 21, at which time she was sold to the English for a huge sum, ransoms being common at the time. At no point during her imprisonment did King

Joan of Arc seen carrying the flag and leading her armies into battle.
(Maryknoll Fathers)

Charles or his subjects make any attempt to rescue her or pay for her ransom. Why Charles ignored Saint Joan is the subject of much speculation. Suffice it to say that she had never been a popular figure in Charles's court, having been adopted only as a last resort. Her earlier prediction was about to prove true: "I will last but a year, scarcely more."

Once Saint Joan was in the hands of the English—a nation still seething from its many losses to her—her execution was widely anticipated. Since the English could not legally condemn her for defeating them in battle, they charged her with heresy and sorcery for refusing to submit to the will of the Church. Tried in Paris by sixty French judges who had sided with their English occupiers, Saint Joan was interrogated many times about her belief that her call came directly from God and not from the Church. (The court records note that she was also charged with stealing a bishop's horse, that her hair was "cut around her ears," and that there was nothing about her "to display and announce her sex, save Nature's own distinctive marks.")

With regard to her visions and the voices she heard, Saint Joan seldom felt the need to defend them. When she was asked about her visions at the trial, court records show that she replied simply, "The angels? Why, they often come among us. Others may not see them, but I do." When she was asked whether Saint Margaret spoke to her in English, she replied, "Why should she speak English? She is not on the English side." When she was asked whether Saint Michael appeared to her in the nude, she said, "Do you think God has not the wherewithal to clothe him?"

Claiming that her call to battle came directly from God and that her actions were taken in His service, Saint Joan was unwilling to place the Church above the explicit directions of her Lord. While the Church was important and sacred to her, she claimed it would always remain secondary to God's demands. "Everything I did, I did on commandment of the Lord," she said during her five-month trial.

Saint Joan was found guilty. The court ruled that her visions had come

The proud man who trusts in himself may fear to undertake anything, but the humble are bold in proportion to the insufficiency of their own which they feel. As they acknowledge their weakness they acquire strength, because they rely on God.
—**SAINT FRANCIS DE SALES**

not from God but from the devil. Her crimes were listed as "heretic, idolater, apostate." Threatened with death, she was tricked into agreeing to submit herself finally to Church authority. But within a few days, she reverted to her original contention that her authority came directly from God. How could she obey the priests when God demanded otherwise? "Never did I a thing against God, nor against the faith."

Saint Joan was sentenced to burn at the stake on May 29, 1431. She met her death with composure, begging God to pardon her judges and all the English people. She asked the priests to say a mass for her while an English soldier made a cross for her from two sticks, which she held tightly to her chest. Her last word was the name "Jesus," which she uttered with a mighty cry. She was nineteen years old.

Twenty-three years after her execution, Saint Joan's mother and two brothers appealed for a reopening of her case. Pope Callistus III appointed a commission for the purpose. On July 7, 1456, the Church decided that Joan had not been given a fair trial. Four hundred and fifty years later, on May 16, 1920, she was canonized.

The Church obviously came to believe that Saint Joan's visions had indeed come directly from God. Yet her visions do raise interesting questions for spiritual seekers. If we have visions, how are we to know when to trust them, when to act on them? How can we tell if they are truly coming from God or His saintly representatives? Are we not in danger of acting on visions that are not Divine but that are the product of unhealthy inner psychological turmoil?

Saint John of the Cross believed that some of our visions are dangerous rather than helpful, for the simple reason that most of us cannot distinguish when God is talking to us from when we are talking to ourselves. He even said that we should probably disregard our visions entirely. Trappist monk Father Thomas Keating, who has a great devotion to Saint John of the Cross, explained to me that Saint John was not entirely opposed to visions and voices but was greatly concerned about the danger of men and

women acting on visions that were contrary to the will of God. Father Keating therefore suggests that we use great caution when interpreting our visions, particularly those that ask us to take some form of radical external action that might negatively affect the lives of others. He also advises us to seek out the wise counsel of a spiritual elder to help us interpret the meaning and significance of our visions.

Whether or not Saint Joan's visions came directly from God is unimportant to me; I am less impressed by supernatural gifts than by extraordinary human willpower. Saint Joan, perhaps more than any other saint, had the will to believe. From the moment she began her audacious mission, she met with doubt and discouragement from every quarter. Yet so strong was her faith in the worth of her mission and the truth of her calling that she persisted against terrible odds. Those of us who have ever been forced to endure a difficult or painful period in our lives know how very hard it is to sustain the kind of unwavering faith that animated Saint Joan. In times of great sadness, when our hearts cry out, "Why, God? Why me?" we are faced with a choice: Do we succumb to our doubts, our despair, and collapse in grief? Or do we cling ever more tenaciously, like Saint Joan, to the belief that despite its trials and tragedies, its horrors and its joys, life is an undeniably glorious experience that should not be squandered on vain or empty pursuits? Give up or move forward; hold fast or let go; believe or disbelieve? The choice is there for all of us—but we must be careful. These choices ultimately define our lives; they are where we find the meaning of our lives.

A PRAYER
TO SAINT JOAN

For Faith

In the face of your enemies, in the face of harassment, ridicule, and doubt, you held firm in your faith. Even in your abandonment, alone and without friends, you held firm in your faith. Even as you faced your own mortality, you held firm in your faith. I pray that I may be as bold in my beliefs as you, St. Joan. I ask that you ride alongside me in my own battles. Help me be mindful that what is worthwhile can be won when I persist. Help me hold firm in my faith. Help me believe in my ability to act well and wisely.

Joan of Arc, preparing to die at the stake.
(Maryknoll Fathers)

10

THE COURAGE
TO CONFRONT

Saint Jerome

When I think of Saint Jerome, I am reminded of the wisdom of something Ralph Waldo Emerson once said: "The next best thing to good preaching is bad preaching." For Saint Jerome was a man of many talents as well as many moods, some of which were angry and utterly self-righteous. Contentious and cantankerous, he took himself and nearly everything he did with utter seriousness. Quick to criticize and slow to forgive, it is hard to imagine a man such as Saint Jerome being canonized in today's world. Yet I find myself strangely attracted to this desert saint, perhaps because I believe I have learned as much from his bad preaching as I have from his good preaching. Saint Jerome was an undeniably human saint because he shouldered and exposed so glaringly many of the imperfections that mar most of our lives. But I have never asked my saints to be angels or gods; I only ask that they have something of value to teach. Saint Jerome has taught me much, not only about the need to confront others occasionally with their flaws but about the danger of doing so without tremendous sensitivity and kindness.

Born about A.D. 340 at Stridon in Dalmatia (part of former Yugoslavia), Saint Jerome was named Eusebius Hieronymus Sophronius, which means "the reverend,

holy-named sage." Like his contemporary, Saint Augustine, he was born to a well-to-do family that furnished him with a first-rate education both in the Latin classics and in Roman religion. This classic education eventually enabled him to spend eighteen years of his life translating the Bible into Latin. Known today as the Vulgate, Saint Jerome's version remains the most influential piece of literature produced during the fourth century. While it is not a perfect translation, it took the Latin language to new heights of beauty and elegance and helped spread the Gospel throughout the Mediterranean world. For this achievement, Saint Jerome was named a Doctor of the Church at his canonization and is known to us today as the patron saint of Bible studies.

Saint Jerome, hermit, scholar, and patron saint of librarians.
(Denver Art Museum)

After a few years of advanced study in Rome—where he acquainted himself with the best of pagan literature, from Cicero to Homer—Saint Jerome returned to Stridon and eventually, in 370, settled in the nearby town of Aquileia, which is today a small seaport but in his time was a large city with vast colonnades and marketplaces and perhaps as many as half a million people. There he and a few friends formed a small ascetic brotherhood. Together they preached a doctrine of extreme asceticism and piety so harsh that it quickly angered the local bishop, Valerian (later Saint Valerian). Valerian questioned the value of extreme asceticism and urged Saint Jerome to become a bit more forgiving and accepting of man's frailties.

Saint Jerome lashed back at Valerian in what would become his characteristic style: personal abuse, followed by rigorous biblical scholarship to make his point. After he had vented his rage, he simply ignored Valerian and returned to his austere ways, save one unshakable habit: He continued to read Cicero, Virgil and other pagan authors, despite the fact that their writings conflicted with his understanding of Christian commitment. It is one of the constant themes of the early Church that it deemed prayer and pagan poetry totally incompatible. Unable to part with his beloved classics, Saint Jerome was a man in conflict.

Perhaps in an effort to solidify his Christian faith, Saint Jerome quite

suddenly left Aquileia, turning his mind and heart toward the desert life-style of Saint Anthony. Together with his companions Innocent, Heliodo-rus, and Hylas, he set off for Jerusalem. All eventually settled at a monastery in the Chalcis desert, near Antioch. The climate, however, proved too harsh for them; Innocent and Hylas died, and Jerome himself fell into a sickness from which he barely recovered. In a letter he later wrote to Saint Eusto-chium, he said that in the heat of fever he fell into a delirium and dreamed he was being arraigned before the judgment seat of Christ. When Christ asked his identity, he answered that he was a Christian. "Thou liest," Christ replied. "Thou art a Ciceronian, not a Christian. For where thy treasure is, there will thy heart be also." As Saint Jerome later wrote, he was deeply

Saint Jerome in his study.
(Giovanni Bellini, National Gallery of Art, London)

shaken: "Straightaway I became dumb, and [then I felt] the strokes of the whip—for He had ordered me to be scourged. . . . At last the bystanders fell at the knees of Him Who presided, and prayed to Him to pardon my youth and give me an opportunity to repent of my error, on the understanding that the extreme torture should be inflicted upon me if ever I read again the books of Gentile authors. . . . This experience was no sweet idle dream. . . . I profess that my shoulders were black and blue, and that I felt the bruises long after I awoke. . . . Henceforth I read the books of God with greater zeal than I had ever given before to the books of men."

After this dream, Jerome would often cry out, "What has Horace to do with the Psalms? Virgil with the Gospels? Cicero with the Apostles? All things are pure to the pure, but we ought not to drink the cup of Christ and the cup of devils." Despite all this, years later Jerome would pay his copyist more for a transcription of Ciceronian dialogue than for a book of homilies.

Saint Augustine shared Saint Jerome's love/hate relationship with the pagan classics. Both saints were divided and tortured souls for much of their early lives because they were unable to reconcile their love for pagan writings with their love for the Gospels. More than any other early Christian saints, Saint Jerome and Saint Augustine were deeply influenced by the classics, which focused more often on the pleasures and pains of the here-and-now than on the glories of the eternal world to come. Unable to draw out the best teachings from pagan writings and apply them to their lives, both saints eventually decided that pagan writings only served to undermine their faith. Yet they both continued throughout their lives to dip into them, incapable of turning their backs on some of the most rich and vibrant prose ever written.

After his recovery, Saint Jerome left the monastery to roam the deserts of northern Egypt. "To me," he once said, "a town is a prison, and the desert loneliness is paradise." He would spend the next four years of his

life in the wilderness of Chalcis as a wandering mendicant, praying, fasting, practicing a variety of forms of self-denial, and studying the Scriptures.

When Saint Jerome finally emerged from the desert in 379, he had learned Hebrew. He went on to be ordained a priest in Antioch—but only on condition that he not be burdened with any particular parish duties because he wanted the life of a recluse. Three years later he was called to Rome, where, serving as the secretary to Pope Damasus I, he was commissioned to produce biblical translations.

While in Rome, Saint Jerome continued to wear the coarse brown robe and tunic of a desert hermit and live the life of an ascetic, all the while surrounded by the luxury of the papal court. His reputation for holiness quickly grew, not only because he became a spiritual adviser to aristocrats and noblewomen practicing the fad of desert asceticism but because the fervent letters he had written in the desert were widely distributed. These letters declared a passion for incorruptibility and spoke of the hermit's life in a way that made it seem exciting. Moreover, in fourth-century life a holy man was a man outside society, and because he was disassociated from petty battles and factions, he was seen as a peacemaker among men. The holy man was regarded as a friend of God, able to wield some influence with the Creator.

It was an age when theological disputes were heated, in which the question of what it meant to be a Christian was endlessly debated. Saint Jerome held firm beliefs that he never lost when it came to the subject of Christian virtue. His popularity plummeted as swiftly as it had risen when he used the debates to criticize passionately the excesses of Roman society. He ridiculed ecclesiastics who spent their time in fashionable company. He condemned the marriage of priests and their frequent sexual transgressions. He blasted the rich clergy and the processions of monsignors. "The only thought of such men is their clothes—are they pleasantly perfumed? Do their shoes fit smoothly?"

Nor did Roman women escape Saint Jerome's venom. "Those women who paint their cheeks with rouge and their eyes with belladonna, whose faces are covered with powder . . . whom no number of years can convince that they are old; who heap their heads with burrowed tresses . . . and behave like trembling schoolgirls before their grandsons . . ."

Soon many people had taken great offense at Saint Jerome's officious piety and biting criticisms of their lifestyle. Some of them, after hearing his sarcastic charge that they "walk on tiptoe so as not to splash their shoes," even proposed to throw him into the Tiber River, along with all the other monks of Rome. But before anyone could make good on that threat, Pope Damasus died in 384. His successor, who did not particularly like Saint Jerome, failed to renew his appointment as secretary. Seven months later, Saint Jerome gathered his beloved books and left Rome forever, headed for the Holy Land. There he was joined later by two of his most ardent women followers, Paula and Eustochium.

Upon their arrival in Bethlehem, Saint Jerome established a monastery. Under his guidance, Paula and Eustochium took up the study of Hebrew and ran a convent. They set up a hospice program for pilgrims visiting the Holy Land and established a school in Bethlehem for young children. Despite Saint Jerome's general mistrust of women (perhaps because he had found them so tempting in his youth), he treated Paula and Eustochium with great respect, placing them in positions of high responsibility.

But Saint Jerome himself was not principally either a social activist or a caregiver—he was a scholar. He set up his own cell in a cave and set to work doing the things he did best—studying, writing, and translating. For the next forty-four years he would produce hundreds of works on biblical interpretation and engage in nearly every important theological debate of his time, often dictating up to a thousand lines a day to his secretaries. Nearly every contemporary Christian thinker, from Saint Augustine to Saint Ambrose, eagerly read his writings.

While it is true that Saint Jerome was indeed an angry, often vindictive

Rash judgment is a spiritual jaundice which makes things appear evil. The cure is to apply love. If your heart is gentle, your judgment will be gentle; if it is loving, so will your judgment be.
—SAINT FRANCIS DE SALES

Saint Jerome

man, he was also capable of great love and dedication. When his follower, Paula, died he was grief stricken. He could be seen beating his chest and crying out loud for mercy. He gave orders for a splendid funeral and wrote an account of her many virtues on the rocks of the cave where she was laid to rest. When he finished, the man who was never lacking for words, would not speak of Paula again, saying only that his "words go on the rocks."

During the last years of Saint Jerome's life, barbarians swept down from the Near East and overran both Syria and Palestine, leaving in their wake tears and destruction. As Saint Jerome wrote, "how many monasteries they captured, how many rivers were reddened with blood . . . The Roman world is falling." He died alone in his cell, emaciated and forlorn, on September 30, 420, while writing a commentary on Jeremiah.

Saint Jerome unquestionably did some bad preaching in his day. For a man who spent his life studying the words of Christ, his intolerant behavior toward others is certainly troubling. It seems to me that he must have forgotten that Jesus once asked us to "Let the man who has no sin on his conscience throw the first stone." The trouble with Saint Jerome's self-righteousness (and all self-righteous people generally) is that he failed to remember that he was as imperfect as those he condemned—he just didn't know it. Rather than look searchingly inside himself to question his motives and the consequences of his angry outbursts, he acted as if he were a pillar of spiritual perfection, incapable of error.

Yet each of us has a duty to confront others from time to time, to take them to task for their less-than-fully human behavior: "If your brother sins [against you], go and tell him his fault between you and him alone. If he listens to you, you have won over your brother" (Matthew 18:15). Saint Thomas More took this passage to heart when he openly complained about the conduct of King Henry VIII and was soon beheaded. Saint Jerome certainly shared that same courage to confront. What he lacked was the sensitivity and compassion to do so in the loving and forgiving manner preached by many of the other saints. And without that sensitivity and true caring for those we confront, what are the chances that they will listen to us? Saint Jerome's greatest shortcoming was that he enjoyed confrontation—perhaps because it provided him with an opportunity to display his stunning intellectual gifts. But confrontation seldom produces positive change when it comes from feelings of anger or from the need to impress others with what we have and they lack.

The great lesson I have taken from Saint Jerome is not that we should avoid all confrontation but that we should never attempt to criticize another unless we first accept them for who they are. As it is said, "God may not love the sin, but he loves the sinner." I now believe that accepting others for who they are is the only basis for love and the starting point for any confrontation aimed at positive change. For where there is no love, there can be no positive change. Love alone changes for the good.

I try to be forgiving of my saints as I try to be of myself. I recognize that Saint Jerome's angry, confrontational style did a great deal of damage to the lives of those he crossed. He was tough. He was critical. He was often self-righteous. Yet I always feel when reading his works and studying his life that he meant well. His zealotry often blinded his vision, and there must be a significant message and warning in this for all of us who hope to become better people. Forgiveness is the essence of it all, and I am more than happy to forgive Saint Jerome, for his contributions far outweighed his angry outbursts. He devoted the bulk of his life to preserving and caring for the documents of the early Church with tremendous energy and in so doing enriched the lives of thousands for more than fourteen centuries. Perhaps his epitaph says it best: "It is not by the brilliance of great men, but by my own strength, that I shall be judged."

A PRAYER
TO SAINT JEROME

For Insight

Through your anger and confrontations you remind us that we all have a duty to confront others from time to time. You also remind us that we have a duty to examine ourselves and confront our own weaknesses and harmful behaviors. Your life teaches that I must accept others for who they are. You taught of the danger of self-righteousness; of the importance of reflecting upon one of Jesus' most insightful teachings: "Let the man who has no sin on his conscience throw the first stone." In the light of your teachings, Saint Jerome, help me to see my own self clearly. Help me to confront my own biases and to act to change others only out of love. If I see that I have the duty to confront another, I ask you to be with me during those necessary but unpleasant moments of confrontation. Help me to remember that love alone can make changes for the good.

11

WE COME BY LOVE AND NOT BY SAIL

Saint Augustine

*F*or the past sixteen hundred years philosophers, evangelists, political scientists, writers, and spiritual seekers have found solace in Saint Augustine's reflections on good and evil, human love, God and Christ, the nature of justice, and the life of faith. Christendom has come to owe him more than any other Church Father. Saint Gregory the Great relied on his works for scriptural commentary and theology, Saint Charlemagne for political theory, Saint Bonaventura for mystical insight, and Saint Thomas Aquinas for elements of scholastic philosophy. Even Dr. Albert Einstein said he profited immensely from reading Augustine's ideas.

Beyond the beauty of his often-captivating prose, I admire Saint Augustine as a passionate man in search of his soul. Few saints have better understood human passion than he; fewer still, the myriad motivations and temptations that haunt us all. His was a quest filled with difficult choices, some poorly made and later repented. Yet ever-present in his life was his quest for communion with God. Saint Augustine was the consummate seeker, never once wavering from his conviction that love is the center of spiritual life and that it must begin by "loving the Love that loved us into existence." In his view, there was no other place to

begin the spiritual quest than in the very center of our silent hearts. Pilgrimages were fine with Saint Augustine; trips to the desert for solitude and reflection were also perfectly acceptable and sometimes even necessary. But he always insisted there was no running away from God. The spiritual life begins at home, he believed, not in some far-off place. As he wrote, "God did not say, go to the east to find wisdom, sail to the west to find justice: there where you seek, you shall find, for to Him who is everywhere present, one comes by love and not by sail."

Saint Augustine was mightily drawn to the beauty of the present, and he was grounded to it through his love of "Him who is everywhere present." As we learn from his autobiography, *Confessions*, he was a sensual man who loved the light, textures, shapes, and colors of the desert landscape of northern Africa. So drawn was he to the beauty of things, to the soulfulness of God's Creation, that he once wrote, "If sensible objects had no soul, one would not love them so much."

Saint Augustine had not begun his life with this mature yet sensuous love of God and His Creation. He had to earn it over a number of tumultuous years of inner struggle. Born into a well-to-do family on November 13, 354, at Tagaste, an agricultural village in northern Africa, he early showed himself to be an extremely intelligent young man. But he hated school because "if I was slow at learning, I was beaten." At the age of sixteen he left Tagaste for Carthage to study Greek, Latin, mathematics, and rhetoric. In Carthage he encountered everything life had to offer and indulged in it with gusto. As he later wrote, "In my youth I burned to get my fill of hellish things. I dared to run wild in different darksome ways of love."

In Carthage, Augustine satisfied his passion by entering into a relationship with a woman to whom he remained faithful for many years but never married. She bore him a son, Adeodatus, in 372. Despite the distractions of his new family, Augustine was able to progress in his studies, and he developed close friendships with three young men: Alypius (a childhood friend from Tagaste), Nebridius, and Honoratus. As he later so sensitively wrote, "What attached me most to my friends was the pleasure of talking and laughing with them, to read with them the same books, to joke and talk nonsense, sometimes to argue, but without anger, and thus to emphasize the pleasure of generally agreeing; to miss an absent friend, to welcome his return. We loved each other with all our hearts, these friendships were expressed by our eyes, our gesture, our voices."

Augustine and his friends engaged in vigorous discussions about theology and the meaning of life, yet struggled to reconcile their love for the pleasures of this world with their love of God. In an effort to resolve this dilemma, Augustine became a follower of Manichaeism, a pseudo-Christian sect that believed in a strict metaphysical dualism. He would later convert Alypius and Honoratus to Manichaeism. According to the Manichees, there were two principles at work in the universe: God, the cause of all good, and matter, the cause of all evil. This dualistic philosophy offered Augustine and his friends an explanation for their own divided souls, yet it only served to divide him further. For nine years Augustine followed the dicta of Manichean thought, which eventually left him "deceived and deceiving," he would later write.

In 383 Augustine left for Rome, where he set up his own school of rhetoric. Finding it difficult to collect his fees, he applied for and won a post as master of rhetoric in Milan, thanks largely to the influence of his Manichean friends. There his reputation as an outstanding teacher grew, along with his finances. By this time his father had died and his mother had come to live with him. She insisted, however, that Augustine give up his mistress and marry a "suitable" wife. He reluctantly agreed, proposed marriage to a new woman, and sent his mistress back to Africa. But his "heart was broken and wounded and shed blood. . . . I was unable to bear the delay of two years which must pass before I was to get the girl I had asked for in marriage. In fact, it was not really marriage that I wanted. I was simply a slave to lust. So I took another woman . . . and thus my soul's disease was nourished and kept alive as vigorously as ever." Increasingly

Saint Augustine, A.D. 354– 430, Doctor of the Church, authored some of the most influential books of Christian theology, among them The City of God, *and* Confessions.

(The Bettmann Archive)

dissatisfied with his life, Augustine longed to heal the divisions within himself, yet still he "panted after honors, gains, marriage."

So the spiritual struggle went on, until one afternoon he was engaged in a discussion at his home with Alypius and Pontitian, a visitor from Africa. Finding a book of Saint Paul's epistles on the table before him, Pontitian began to share with Augustine and Alypius the story of two men who had converted to Christianity after reading the story of Saint Anthony. Pontitian then got up to take a stroll in the garden, and Saint Augustine joined him. He walked past Pontitian deep into the garden and then stopped under the comforting shade of a fig tree. Once alone, Augustine threw himself to the ground and cried out loud, "How long, O Lord? Wilt thou be angry forever? Remember not my past iniquities!" Then he heard the voice of a child singing from a neighboring house: "Take up and read! Take up and read!" "At this I looked up, thinking hard whether there was any kind of game in which children used to chant words like these, but I could not remember ever hearing them before. I stemmed my flood of tears and stood up, telling myself that this could only be a divine command to open my book of Scripture and read the first passage on which my eyes should fall."

Augustine returned to where Alypius was sitting with the book of Saint Paul's epistles, opened it at random, and began to read Romans 13:13: "Not in rioting and drunkenness, not in chambering and wantonness, not in strife and envying: but put ye on the Lord Jesus Christ, and make not provision for the flesh, to fulfill its lusts." After reading the words that would change his life, he closed the book and shared with Alypius what had just occurred. "I had no wish to read more and no need to do so," wrote Augustine. "For in an instant, as I came to the end of the sentence, it was as though the light of confidence flooded into my heart and all the darkness of doubt dispelled." Alypius asked to see the epistles and turned his gaze to another passage: "Him that is weak in faith, take unto you." Overcome with emotion, Augustine and Alypius made a decision to convert to Christianity. On Easter eve in 387, Augustine and Alypius were baptized by Saint Ambrose.

In September 388, Augustine returned to his home in Africa, where he would spend the next thirty years of his life writing almost constantly. The three works that brought him the most enduring fame were his autobiographical *Confessions;* his defense of Christian theology, *On the Trinity;* and his theological response to the sacking of Rome, *The City of God,* one of the most influential books of theology ever written.

To gain a sense of appreciation for *The City of God,* imagine the message of hope it must have imparted to those living in northern Africa in the year

You ask, "Why should I not love the world, since God made it?" Brethren, a man loves God too little who loves anything except for God's sake: it is not that created things may not be loved, but to love them for themselves is cupidity, not love.

—SAINT AUGUSTINE

410. In that year Saint Augustine first received the news that Alaric the Goth and his barbarians had sacked Rome. The first thing he did was reassure his terrified followers, who were convinced the world was about to end: "If this catastrophe is indeed true, it must be God's will. Men build cities and men destroy cities, but the city of God they didn't build and cannot destroy." He went on to tell them, "The heavenly city outshines Rome beyond comparison. There instead of victory is truth; instead of high rank, holiness; instead of peace, felicity; instead of life, eternity. . . . Pythagoras said this, Plato said that. Put them near the Rock, and compare these arrogant people with Him who was crucified. Thus we come to see in our fallen state, our imperfection, that we can conceive perfection. Through the Incarnation, the presence of God among us and the lineaments of man, we have a window in the walls of time which looks out onto this heavenly city." In essence, what Saint Augustine said to his flock was that they had nothing to worry about so long as they humbly submitted themselves to the will of God.

The humility that Saint Augustine prized is obviously not a virtue that we greatly treasure in the modern world, where so much of our lives is dominated by the belief that we can control and alter our destiny through new medical and technological breakthroughs. In *The City of God,* Saint Augustine argued that we are not the all-powerful race we proclaim ourselves to be. His message was a warning not only about the danger of human pride, so prevalent in our own time, but that all of our creations are ultimately perishable. As a Christian, Saint Augustine said that he had no continuing earthly city. He was not the citizen of a city built by man, but the citizen of a city built by God. For the city of man is temporal and perishable, while the city of God is eternal and glorious.

Many of the images and advertisements of our commercial world ask us to pursue wealth, celebrity, and power rather than the humble and contrite hearts Saint Augustine encouraged us to cultivate. If Saint Augustine were alive and preaching today, I suspect he would wake us up to the realization that happiness is found not in the pursuit of pleasure but in the pursuit of goodness—which begins with the desire to serve God first. The entire history of the saints is really a chronicle of this alternative quest for truth and goodness down the road less traveled.

Saint Augustine insisted that Christian history is an open rather than a closed book. He was convinced that Christianity would survive so long as a few men and women fixed their hearts on the city of God instead of the city of man. Numerous nations have risen and fallen into oblivion since Saint Augustine's death, yet men and women dominated by the love of God continue to dwell among us, daily working miracles in the spirit of Christ. Blessed Father Damian of Molaki, Albert Schweitzer, and Martin Luther King, Jr., were all inspired by the same beautiful vision that drove Saint Augustine, a vision that encouraged them to advance their spiritual growth through love rather than power, humility rather than arrogance, hope rather than despair. They did not live their lives on the shifting sands of changing morals and passing fads but on the eternal values of the city of God. Their only goal was to seek "Him who is everywhere," by love and not by sail.

A PRAYER
TO SAINT AUGUSTINE

For Unity with God and Nature

Saint Augustine is the patron saint of brewers and printers. The city of St. Augustine, Florida (the oldest city in America), was named in his honor, the Spanish having first landed there on his feast day, August 28, 1565.
(Antonio Rodriguez, Denver Art Museum)

You were a sensuous man who was often tormented by natural appetite and desire. You found your way to God through your stronger desire to live a spiritual life rich with meaning. Help me to see as you taught, that God is everywhere present for those who are willing to seek Him, and for those who are willing to love Him as He loves us. Help me to see through my desires to God, and help me to see God's love for me in my desires. I ask you, Saint Augustine, to help me find God in all that I see. Flood my spirit with the desire to know and love God with all my heart.

12

A FAITH
THAT LIFTS THE
STAGGERING SOUL

—

Mother Elizabeth Seton

*I*n 1952, when Ann Hooe was just four and a half years old and dying of leukemia, her parents drove her northwest from Baltimore to visit the tomb of Elizabeth Seton in Emmitsburg, Maryland. At the time, the nuns of the Daughters of Charity were preparing the case for Elizabeth's beatification. They were searching for miracles to credit to the founder of their order, so they asked Ann's mother, Felixena Ann O'Neill, if she would be kind enough to direct her prayers to Elizabeth Seton. No one in the family expected the young girl to survive, but they all agreed that a few prayers to Elizabeth were at least worth a try. Within one week of their visit to Elizabeth Seton's tomb and a great many prayers, Ann's blood count was normal.

When Ann stayed cancer-free for nine years, the Archdiocese of Baltimore was convinced that a miracle had occurred, so they sent the news to the Vatican. In 1963, after lengthy study, Pope John XXIII agreed: A miracle had occurred through the intercession of Elizabeth Seton. In 1975, Pope Paul VI canonized Elizabeth Seton, making her the first native-born American saint.

Now a forty-five-year-old grandmother, Ann Hooe remains convinced that Saint Elizabeth Seton saved her life. "It was definitely a miracle," she recently told a

Elizabeth Bailey (1794)
miniature at the time of her
marriage to William Seton.
(Seton Shrine Center)

newspaper. Her devotion to Saint Elizabeth has never wavered since that time, and she is joined today by the hundreds of men and women who have been drawn to this unusually courageous and sturdy woman, a saint who survived the deaths of her husband and two teenage daughters, yet somehow never grew bitter.

Of all the saints I have studied, Saint Elizabeth Seton has given me the most insight into coping with family tragedies. Her life is truly a lesson in tenacity, resilience, and spiritual fortitude. She found her way back from the petrifying edge of tragedy through, as she once wrote, "a faith that lifts the staggering soul on one side" and "hope which supports it on the other." Despite the tragedies that plagued her, her vision of the sacred in all of life held firm. After her daughters' deaths she built the religious order, the Daughters of Charity, and firmly established the parochial school system in America. How she managed to blend motherhood with sisterhood is a lesson in the art of balance, faith, and the power of an unbendable will.

Vastly different from the wandering mendicant saints of the Middle Ages or the scholarly recluses of Europe, Mother Seton, as she came to be called, was married and bore five children. Born in New York City in 1774 to Dr. Richard Bailey, a successful surgeon, and his wife, Catherine, young Elizabeth was born to a life of privilege. Three years later, however, her mother died.

At the age of nineteen, Elizabeth married William Magee Seton, a wealthy merchant and a devout Episcopalian like herself. What followed were ten years of happy marriage and the birth of five children. Quite suddenly, however, Mr. Seton's business began to fail, and he contracted tuberculosis. In an effort to cure the disease, Mr. Seton's doctor advised him and Elizabeth to take a sea voyage to Italy. So the young couple and their eldest daughter, Anna Maria, immediately set sail for Italy. Upon their arrival, however, they were quarantined for thirty days for fear of a yellow fever outbreak. That confinement proved fatal to the ailing William Seton, for not long after their release, he died. Within forty-eight hours he was buried in Pisa, leaving Elizabeth a twenty-nine-year-old widow with five children to support.

During the fifty-six-day voyage back to America, Elizabeth was joined by a family friend, Antonio Fulicchi, who urged her to convert to Catholicism. Antonio was apparently a very persuasive man, for within one year of her return to America and against the staunch opposition of her family and friends, she became a Catholic in 1805. As she wrote in a letter to Fulicchi at the time, "Here my God go I, heart all to you . . . these are my happiest days."

Within a short time after her conversion, Elizabeth began a school for boys. Almost immediately, it failed. She then opened up a school for girls adjoining St. Mary's Seminary in Baltimore, which was successful. What Elizabeth most wanted was to found an order of Catholic women and become a nun, but she thought rearing her children made this impossible. Father William Du Bourg, the rector at St. Mary's Seminary, thought otherwise. He saw no reason why Elizabeth could not be both a mother and a nun, and within a month of her arrival in Baltimore, he urged her to establish the Daughters of Charity of Saint Vincent de Paul. "It is expected I shall be the mother of many daughters," she wrote.

The first steps toward the establishment of the sisterhood were taken in 1809, when provisional guidelines were adopted and Father Du Bourg was appointed director. On June 2 of that year, Elizabeth Seton donned the habit, "a long black robe with a cape, and a white cap with a crimped border." She was joined by four other women, each of whom took vows of poverty, chastity, and obedience in the presence of the archbishop. The new community was named the Daughters of Saint Joseph, and Elizabeth was appointed its mother superior.

Within three weeks of her new appointment, Mother Seton moved her family and the fledgling order to Emmitsburg, fifty miles from Baltimore, where a farm was purchased for the establishment of a school. The school itself was opened in 1810, the first parochial school in the United States.

After a rough beginning, Mother Seton's school slowly began to grow. As she wrote of herself, "while the world thinks she is deprived of everything worth having . . . she has truly and really the best of it." Her happiness was short-lived, however, for later that same year she lost her daughter Anna Maria to tuberculosis. Her grief was severe and longstanding, yet she managed to cope, perhaps because, as she wrote at the time, "sickness and death itself, if it comes to us again, we know that they are the common attendants of human life. They are our certain portion at one period or other, and it would be madness to be unhappy because I am treated like the rest of human beings."

Children of Elizabeth Ann Seton.
(Seton Shrine Center)

Annina 1795-1812

Rebecca 1802-1816

Richard 1798-1823

Catherine 1800-1891

William 1796-1868

By 1813, eighteen sisters were living in Mother Seton's convent, as well as thirty-two paying boarders. In 1814 she sent her sisters to take charge of an orphanage in Philadelphia, the first Catholic institution of its kind in the country. Shortly after these triumphs, in 1816, Mother Seton's youngest daughter, Rebecca, died of tuberculosis—"the family enemy," as she had come to call the disease. Mother Seton buried both of her daughters in the nearby woods of her convent property in a place where she could gaze down at their graves from her room. She wrote that "twenty times a day— first thing in the morning and last thing at night"—she peered out that window and thought "of those beautiful and joyous souls." And increasingly, Elizabeth thought of her own ultimate death as well, for she too had contracted tuberculosis. As she wrote to a friend at the time, "Oh, Eliza, how many strings draw us up as well as downward. . . . I shall be free bye and bye, and able to go in my turn without one string to pull me back."

Despite the many tragedies that befell Mother Seton, her poor health, and the ongoing task of rearing her remaining children, she continued to minister to the needs of the convent. By 1817, she managed to open a second orphanage in New York, and before her death in 1823 at the age of forty-six, she prepared plans for a Catholic hospital in Baltimore. That hospital would open just a few years later. Her Daughters of Charity would go on to pick up the wounded on Civil War battlefields, teach in schools across America at nearly every level, and found hospitals, homes for the aged, orphanages, and schools for the deaf. Today the Daughters of Charity serve in both North and South America as well as in Italy and on a variety of foreign missions.

Saint Elizabeth Seton once said, "We must be so careful to meet our grace. If mine depended on going to a place to which I had the most dreadful aversion, in that place there is a store of grace waiting for me— what a comfort." I believe what she meant by this is that each event in our

*T*he Church of God needs
saints today. This imposes a
great responsibility on us.
We must become holy, not
because we want to feel
holy, but because Christ
must be able to live His life
fully in us.
　　　—MOTHER TERESA
　　　　OF CALCUTTA

lives, no matter how pleasant or unpleasant, presents us with opportunities for spiritual growth. "We must be so careful to meet our grace"—this means that suffering opens doors to God, just as surely as does joy. Saint Elizabeth somehow came to see that one of the reasons we grow bitter or angry is that we feel that we haven't gotten what we deserve. We are always happy to accept the "good graces," but how many of us are ready to accept the "bad graces"? Saint Elizabeth Seton never had the need to categorize grace because she never fell into the trap of asking for more than she got. She placed her trust in God and left it at that. "Thy will be done," she said at the graveside service of her daughter Anna Maria. She saw no sense in asking "Why, God?" only in asking "How can I grow from this?" Her fervent lifelong prayer truly was "Thy will be done," and she proved her faith through nearly every action of her life. While she experienced great suffering, she never grew bitter because she came to see that without suffering we cannot understand love.

"Tribulation is my element," Mother Seton once said. She confronted the same challenge we all face: She could either grow from her sufferings or let them destroy her. She chose to see beyond the suffering and to develop a deeper sense of compassion. That sense of compassion continues to drive the work of the Daughters of Charity today as a testament to what one saddened heart can accomplish.

More than any other saint, Mother Seton has taught me that all of us act and react throughout our lives to a variety of occurrences that are beyond our control. She often stressed that what is important is not so much what happens to us but how we perceive and respond to what happens to us. As Rabbi Harold Kushner once wrote, "It is not a matter of whether we look at a glass and see it as half empty. It is whether faith and experience have taught us to look at a glass that is nearly empty . . . and believing that there are resources in the world capable of refilling it." Mother Seton never saw an empty glass—only glasses that forever needed filling.

We all begin our day with a sunrise. Some may see the day's beginning as just another Monday. Others will witness the sunrise and pause to admire its beauty and relish the sanctity of life in that moment. I think of Saint Seton as a woman who often paused to thank God for the sacred in her everyday world, despite the many griefs that befell her. Through her suffering she learned about love, and through her love she served God with all the faith and hope she had. What more could we possibly ask of a saint?

A PRAYER
TO ELIZABETH SETON

For Constancy and Comfort

Your life was full of immense suffering, yet you maintained your faith. Even during your deepest sorrows, you served others. You said, "Tribulation is my element," and saw beyond your suffering and into others. I would ask you, Mother Seton, to stand with me when I hurt the most. Help me develop compassion—compassion for my suffering and, through it, compassion for the wounds and sorrows that all other people hold. Show me the path through my sufferings that will lead me to know more love, and through that love know more about God.

This portrait of Mother Seton belonged to her close friend, Antonio Fulicchi, the man who urged her to convert to Catholicism.
(Seton Shrine Center)

13

A BROTHERHOOD
OF JOY

Saint Francis of Assisi

*U*npretentious, sensuous, and always at home in the company of the disadvantaged and the dispossessed, Saint Francis (1181–1226) served God less with his mind than with his heart. He was able to recognize the Divine spark in everyone he met, from the disease-ravaged face of a leper to the war-scarred face of a fallen knight. His spiritual mission was the care of souls, and in accepting that mission he became one of the most admired monks, missionaries, and mystics in the history of the Church.

Saint Francis lives on today in the work of the thousands of Franciscan friars who have devoted their lives to the service of others. One such contemporary Franciscan is Father Marty Wolf of Colorado, who draws strength from Saint Francis's example in his work with the poor. "I've seen the face of God in the poor," he once told me. "And now I see God's face in the eyes of the people I serve who have AIDS. Leprosy was the AIDS of Francis's time, and a leper played an important role in Francis's conversion to Christianity. Saint Francis came across a leper while walking along a road and greeted him warmly, despite his initial fear. Then he felt called by God to kiss him. I feel quite strongly that if Saint Francis lived today he would be as loving with those who have AIDS as he was with

Although this picture depicts a somber Saint Francis, the passionate ascetic and mystic was almost never somber.
(Zurbarán, National Gallery of Art, London)

that leper. He was always a champion of the poor and the rejected. He serves as an inspiration to me each and every day that I live. He gives me the courage to carry on."

In his autobiographical "Testament," Saint Francis confirms Father Wolf's understanding of the Franciscan mission in his own words: "During my life of sin, nothing disgusted me like seeing victims of leprosy. It was the Lord Himself who urged me to go to them. I did so, and ever since, everything was so changed for me that what had seemed at first painful and impossible to overcome became easy and pleasant. Shortly after, I definitely forsook the world."

Saint Francis found his way to this mission of compassion through a natural and rather slow conversion, moving from a youth spent daydreaming of knighthood to a manhood devoted to rebuilding the fallen walls of a corrupt Church. He was born in Assisi, Italy, either in late 1181 or early 1182. Although he eventually learned to read and write, Saint Francis often called himself an *"idiota,"* recognizing that the only thing he had mastered as a youth was the ability to spend his wealthy father's money foolishly and lavishly although often quite generously. The residents of Assisi considered him a spoiled but likable young dandy who was fond of singing, joking, and drinking. In the words of Saint Bonaventura, an early biographer of Saint Francis, he was "nurtured in vanity among the vain sons of men."

Saint Francis had been nurtured not only in vanity but in the dream of one day becoming a glorious knight. This longing was born from the frequent visits of famous French troubadours, who wandered through Italy rhyming the legendary history of Charlemagne and the Knights of the Round Table. Francis's father, Pietro Bernadone, a wealthy cloth merchant, shared his young son's dream. With his help, in fact, Saint Francis tried several times to become a knight by distinguishing himself in battle. But all his attempts were frustrated, and his father became convinced that his son was both a coward and a fool.

Not until Saint Francis's twenty-fifth birthday did he begin his journey toward God, but he was as unsure how to become a man of faith as he had been to become a man of the sword. His first attempt was to give away money at such a madcap rate that his family and neighbors began to fear that he had gone mad.

Tormented by the ridicule of his family and friends, Saint Francis became increasingly depressed. For solace he often retreated to a secluded cavern to cry over his sins and pray for spiritual direction. Although full of compassion and a desire to serve God, he did not know how. What did God want from him? The answer to this question finally crystallized for the young saint one day while he was walking in the Italian countryside. He stopped at an ancient church in San Damiano that was falling into disrepair. Here, as he prayed at the foot of a crucifix, Christ spoke directly to him, saying only, "Francis, repair my house."

Determined to take Christ's words literally, Saint Francis immediately ran home, grabbed a bundle of his father's precious cloth, and sold it in the town market. He then sold his horse and made his way back to San Damiano on foot. He pleaded with the parish priest of the small church to take the money, but the priest, thinking him crazy, refused. Saint Francis flung the money into a corner of the church and ran. After arguing and finally breaking with his father over this impetuous venture, Saint Francis begged in the streets for the materials he needed to rebuild San Damiano. It was April 1206, and Saint Francis had finally taken his first step toward a life in service of God.

Saint Francis met with immediate success in his reconstruction efforts. Soon he even had a small group of men willing to aid him, first at San Damiano, then at several other churches. The men were attracted by Saint Francis's simplicity, love of nature, joyous spirit, and complete devotion to poverty. In the eyes of his followers, he was a holy man in an unholy time living a total commitment to the second commandment: Love thy neighbor.

Supported vigorously by his followers, Saint Francis became a man at peace with himself, yet he soon realized his life's work was to "rebuild God's house" far beyond the borders of Assisi. He envisioned himself as the head of a great army of men and women devoted to spiritual life. With his sense of humor and laughing spirit, he would obviously be an easy man to follow.

By all accounts Saint Francis was an inspired speaker. Many of those who heard him said they felt he was talking especially to them, even when he addressed a large crowd. He always spoke only of love, never threatening his listeners with words of hell and damnation. He spoke of their sins as if each sinner were his own son or daughter, as if the thought of their personal failures broke his heart. As Thomas, Archdeacon of Spoleto, wrote:

> In that year [1222], I was residing in the Studium of Bologna; on the feast of the Assumption, I saw Saint Francis preach in the public square in front of the public palace. The theme of his sermon was: "Angels, men, and demons." He spoke so well and with such sterling clarity on these three classes of spiritual and rational beings that the way in which this untutored man developed his subject aroused even among the scholars in the audience an admiration that knew no bounds. . . .
>
> He was wearing a ragged habit; his whole person seemed insignificant; he did not have an attractive face. But God conferred so much power on his words that they brought back peace in many a seignorial family torn apart until then by old, cruel, and furious hatreds even to the point of assassinations. The people showed him as much respect as they did devotion; men and women flocked to him; it was a question of who would at least touch the fringe of his clothing or who would tear off a piece of his poor habit.

In Saint Francis's time priests generally spoke to their congregations in formal language and often relied on the homilies of the Fathers of the Church for their subject matter. Saint Francis, on the other hand, urged his brothers to preach a simple, easily digested theology of love. He and his brothers took their message to the town squares of Italy and Europe, conducting hundreds of heart-to-heart talks with their listeners, not unlike street evangelists of our own time. After hearing one of Saint Francis's sermons, Stephen of Bourbon wrote that he brought "wholesome shame and great edification of his hearers."

When Saint Francis had several dedicated followers, he decided it was time to gain papal approval for his new brotherhood of friars. Yet when he quietly presented himself to Pope Innocent III for verbal approval of his Rule in April or May 1209, he met with a cool reception. The Pope was daily besieged by any number of self-appointed reformers in search of his blessing. Why should he take Saint Francis seriously? As one of Saint Francis's biographers, Matthew of Paris, reports, Pope Innocent III was nearly belligerent to the humble friar. "Leave me alone with your Rule!" he shouted. "Go find your pigs instead! You can preach all the sermons you want to them." Upon hearing this order, Saint Francis turned and went to find the nearest pigsty, where he smeared himself with dung and returned to the Pope's offices. A surprised Innocent III decided that at least Saint Francis was not a rebel, so he granted him conditional approval for the new order, which was to be named Friars Minor. As Saint Francis later wrote in his "Testament":

> When God gave me some friars, there was no one to tell me what I should do; but the Most High Himself made it clear to me that I must live the life of the Gospel. I had this written down briefly and simply and his Holiness the Pope confirmed it for me.

As for the actual "Rule" that Saint Francis presented to the pontiff, history leaves us with few records of its exact contents. All we know is that it was very short and consisted of Gospel texts and a few regulations. We know that the brothers were to wear a tunic with a hood, a cord, and pants underneath. They were to be admitted to the brotherhood only after aban-

If I were to see the emperor, I would beg him to command that grain be scattered on the roads at Christmas to regale the birds, especially our sisters the larks.

—SAINT FRANCIS OF ASSISI

doning all their goods and giving them to the poor. Yet the most significant aspect of the Rule was its emphasis that all brothers take a vow of poverty. While the Benedictine Rule had recognized limited communal property, Saint Francis set the ideal of absolute poverty for both the community and the individual. As Saint Bonaventura would write of Saint Francis, "From the first moment of his religious life until his death, his sole wealth consisted in a habit, a cord, and a pair of trousers."

Through his poverty and simplicity, Saint Francis came fully to appreciate the beauty of the Divine in every aspect of Creation. He found the world and its earthly pleasures wonderful and beautiful to behold. He never tired of looking out over the delicate landscapes of Italy or listening to the morning song of larks. His temperament was that of an artist, not a world-forsaking philosopher. His love of nature inspired much of his poetry, as in this phrase, taken from his famed "Canticle of Brother Sun": "Be praised, My Lord, for our sister water / useful and humble, precious and clear. Be praised, My Lord, for our brother fire / through whom light comes in darkness / He is bright and pleasant, mighty and robust."

By 1217, bands of Friars Minor were living in Italy, France, Spain, Bohemia, Germany, England, and the Holy Land. The growth of the Friars Minor was startling, so startling, in fact, that Saint Francis felt the need finally to see his order of brothers formally recognized by the Church. He struggled to write a new Rule that would unite his followers, who were increasingly agitating for new leadership and change. After a frustrating effort, he resigned himself to letting his fellow brothers and a liaison to the Pope work over the Rule until it passed as detailed monastic legislation. In November 1223, Pope Honorius III approved it as the official legislation of the Friars Minor.

Once freed from the responsibility of seeing the brotherhood officially recognized, Saint Francis settled in La Verna, Italy, where he climbed a nearby hill and had a small "cell" built to which he could retreat daily for prayer. We know something of what happened during these retreats largely

because Brother Leo "spied" on Saint Francis and recorded what he saw. His witness was later retold by Thomas of Celano. The portrait Brother Leo paints is of a humble man who often worried about the future of his brotherhood. "Lord," he would often ask, "what will become of this poor little family that You have entrusted to me, when I am gone?"

Toward the end of his life, Saint Francis told Brother Leo that something wonderful was about to happen. And on the night of September 14, 1224, Saint Francis was marked with the stigmata—the marks of Christ's wounds as He hung from the cross, the first officially recognized appearance of the stigmata in the history of the Church. On this night, a seraph bearing the mark of the cross descended upon Saint Francis and left him with the wounds. Legend has it that the entire region saw a bright light on the summit near Saint Francis's cave. "His whole soul thirsted for Christ and he dedicated to him his body as well as his heart," wrote Thomas of Celano.

Shortly after receiving the stigmata, Saint Francis's health deteriorated rapidly. He suffered from tuberculosis and nearly went blind. His friend Cardinal Ugolino insisted that he see a doctor at the hermitage of Fonte Columbo. When he refused, the cardinal ordered him to oblige. As Saint Francis never went against an order of the Church, he reluctantly agreed to undergo treatment for his blindness. The doctor prescribed a treatment of cauterization from his earlobe to his temple. As the doctor heated the rod, Saint Francis began to pray: "My Brother Fire, the Most High has given you a splendor that all other creatures envy. Show yourself to be kind and courteous to me. . . . I pray the Magnificent Lord to temper his fiery heat so that I may have the strength to bear the burning caress." With that, the doctor began his "treatment." Saint Francis never flinched, and when it was over, he noted teasingly, "If it's not cooked enough, you may begin again." The treatment was a failure, but it hardly mattered—Saint Francis's health now was beyond repair. His liver and stomach had begun to fail.

On the eve of Saint Francis's death, larks were said to have poured from

the sky to sing their song, which they usually sang only in the morning. The next day, after singing his last prayer, the humble saint went silent. The date was October 3, 1226, and Saint Francis was forty-six years old. His body was taken to Assisi for burial at Saint George's Church. Two years later, on July 16, 1228, he was canonized at Assisi by Pope Gregory IX.

Saint Francis seems to have been a man who truly found happiness, or perhaps whom happiness found. While every saint is a man or woman of heroic determination, Saint Francis had unusual confidence in the strength of the individual to create a life rich with meaning. He taught his followers not only how to love but how to sing and laugh like a jester, infusing the religious experience with new-found joy. He told them that "spiritual joy is as necessary to the soul as blood to the body." He radiated this teaching, bringing bliss to all who came in contact with him.

What was the secret to Saint Francis's sense of fulfillment? He strived to live each moment as a gift, as a blessing. He made spiritual life quite simple. He did not need to read or contemplate great theological doctrines or philosophical tracts, not because he couldn't understand them but because he came to see that simple gratefulness was all that he needed. Saint Francis believed that as long as we live each moment as a gift and remain in a state of endless fascination, endless appreciation, and endless love, fulfillment is our natural destiny.

Few of us are able to remain in the state of perpetual gratitude that animated Saint Francis's life. It is so easy to slip into states of anger, pettiness, ungratefulness. The cure? Saint Francis had a ready answer: Pray harder, for prayerfulness leads to gratefulness. Through prayer we return to a state of heartfelt appreciation for life.

A PRAYER TO
FRANCIS OF ASSISI

For Joy and Gratitude

Gentle Saint of poverty and humility, you have taught how very important it is to sing and laugh. "Spiritual Joy," you said, "is as necessary to the soul as blood to the body." I would ask you, Saint Francis, to bring more humor and lightness into my life, to lift up my soul with warmth and gaiety. Help me to realize the worship of God in my celebration of the present moment, in my laughter. Help me to express my gratitude, and through my own laughter and happiness to lift the hearts of my loved ones.

Saint Francis of Assisi, depicted in a Mexican bulto carving by Miguel Herrera.
(Denver Art Museum)

14

THIS MISSION
OF LOVE

———

Mother Frances Cabrini

*W*hen once asked to define a missionary, Mother Frances Cabrini responded by comparing her work to that of a candle, for "the missionary radiates light while she consumes her life embracing everything—labors, joys, and pains—for the salvation of all people."

Today, Mother Cabrini's candle continues to glow in the work of fifty-six-year-old Mary MacKinnon, who in 1992 joined the Cabrini Mission Corps, which was recently established to serve as an outreach program for lay people. Members of the Mission Corps devote at least one year of their lives to serving the neediest members of society. As Mary recently told me, "One of the things that appealed to me about Mother Cabrini was that she was always encouraging lay people to get involved in missionary work. And like her, I have always been drawn to social service of one kind or another. My only problem was that the financial needs of my family prevented me from considering such a move until I was fifty-five years old, for it wasn't until that time that my financial pressures eased with an early retirement plan I accepted from the Gillette Company in Boston."

Mary MacKinnon can be found today in her temporary home at the Missionary Sisters of the Sacred

Heart Convent in Manhattan. Each morning she leaves the convent to walk around the east side of Manhattan, where she makes her daily rounds to a group of twenty elderly people who range in age from fifty-six to ninety-four. She does whatever she can for her elderly friends, helping with banking transactions, cooking meals, cleaning, or simply making herself available for conversation. "I want to make a difference in the lives that I touch," says Mary. "I feel that the small things I accomplish do make a difference. I have had a terrific life, and giving back a bit of the joy I've received is tremendously enriching. I view this life as a pilgrimage, you know, and I strongly believe that we are our brother's keeper. And the more we give of ourselves, the more splendid this pilgrimage becomes."

Mother Frances Cabrini
(Maryknoll Fathers)

Mother Cabrini shared Mary's belief. In the span of her career as a missionary nun, she founded sixty-seven charitable institutions and convents under the auspices of her order, the Missionary Sisters of the Sacred Heart. That she did so with such remarkable skill and charity earned her sainthood in 1946. On the occasion of her canonization, Pope Pius XII said of her works that "while human beings are transitory and all grow old little by little and fall in ruin, the glories, the initiatives and the works which flow from Christian holiness, on the other hand, not only are preserved with the passage of time but prosper and flourish, sustained by a marvelous force."

Pope Pius was surely correct. The "works which flow from Christian holiness" do indeed live on, and this is especially so with the works of Mother Cabrini. Seventy-six years after her death, her compassion for the poor and the dispossessed can be seen not only in the work of Mary but in the eyes of the thousands of patients who are cared for in the three hospitals she established in the United States. Cabrini Medical Center, for instance, a 499-bed community teaching hospital in New York, celebrated its centennial in 1992 by renewing its dedication to serving those most in need of care, including the elderly, the poor, and those stricken with AIDS.

• • •

Mother Cabrini was born in 1850 in a tiny village on the Lombard plain of Italy. Although small and frail as a girl, she was captivated by missionaries' tales of adventure, heroism, and compassion in faraway lands. She was particularly fascinated with the Orient and longed to become a missionary to China. By the time she came of age to join an order, however, no one would take her on account of her frail health.

When Frances Cabrini was thirty and had become a teacher, the Bishop of Lombardy asked her to run a small orphanage for girls called the House of Providence, in the town of Codogno. The orphanage had become an embarrassment to the Church because years earlier, the local parish had agreed to let a woman operate it, but she turned out to have kept the children ill fed and in rags.

Frances Cabrini accepted the bishop's proposal without any idea of the true situation at the orphanage. When she entered the House of Providence, she found an antagonistic headmistress and a host of frightened children living in squalor. The first thing Frances did was write her sister to ask for much-needed medical supplies and fabric. She then began to clean up the large room where the girls' beds were lined against the walls. The headmistress railed at Cabrini day and night, often bringing her to tears—tears Frances would later confess she was ashamed of. But she persisted with her work, teaching the girls mathematics, reading, and geography, and she shared with them her belief that work is a means of expressing devotion to God.

During her three years at the House of Providence, Frances never let go of her desire to become a nun. Her persistent and headstrong ways at the orphanage finally convinced the bishop that she was a fit candidate for the convent. He finally agreed to let her become a nun, and seven of the orphaned girls joined her in taking the vow of poverty, obedience, and celibacy.

The newly ordained nuns continued to work at the House of Providence, but after a few months Frances presented evidence to the bishop that the headmistress was stealing money from the parish, and she demanded the bishop intercede in the matter. After hearing the evidence, the bishop dissolved the orphanage and advised Frances to form a missionary order of nuns. "I shall search for a house," the stunned Cabrini replied. The year was 1880. Within seven years, the ambitious Mother Cabrini founded six additional convents.

Satisfied with her success in Italy, Mother Cabrini decided it was time to act on her dream of becoming a missionary to China. She sought an audience with Pope Leo XIII to gain permission for her planned missionary work. But instead of meeting with the Pope, Mother Cabrini was interviewed by Cardinal-Vicar Parocchi, who requested that she open two institutions in Rome—a free school and a nursery. "Neither men, circumstances, nor devils can stop me now," she declared, delighted with her new mission. She raised a small amount of money for the new ventures and found more nuns to staff her operations. Once these institutions were successfully under way, she again petitioned the Vatican for permission to travel to China. Instead, she was ordered to bring her mission to New York to help the Italian immigrants struggling to make a new life in the United States.

"My daughter, your field awaits you not in the East but in the West. Frances Cabrini, go to America," Pope Leo XIII told her. So in 1889 she sailed for New York. When she arrived, there was no one to greet her. She had been told that a group of Scalabrinian Fathers had started an orphanage in New York, and she understood that she and her nuns were to operate the institution. After finding her way to the Scalabrinian monastery, she was told the orphanage existed only in the priests' dreams. To make things worse, there was no place for her or her nuns to stay at the monastery, so they spent the night in the cheapest accommodations they could find, taking turns staying awake to keep the rats off one another. The following

Charity and devotion differ no more than the flame from the fire. Charity is a spiritual fire which breaks out into flame and is then called devotion.
—SAINT FRANCIS DE SALES

day, they went to the archbishop's residence and were told regretfully that they must return to Rome. Mother Cabrini refused. "America is my ordained mission," she told the astonished archbishop. "Excellence, in all humbleness, I must say, in America I stay."

And stay she did. That year, a New York newspaper reported, "These young nuns hardly speak English. The Directoress of their congregation is 'Madre Francesca Cabrini', a diminutive, youthful lady with great eyes and an attractive smiling face. She does not know the English language, but she knows the universal language of the human spirit."

Mother Cabrini eventually taught herself English even as she and her sisters threw themselves into assisting the thousands of Italian immigrants pouring into New York City. Conditions for these immigrants were brutal, and Mother Cabrini was determined to improve their lot by establishing an orphanage for the many suffering children. The situation is described in the foreword to *The Life of Mother Cabrini*: "Stuffed into foul tenements, not knowing the language or how to escape their New World prisons, many [Italian immigrants], especially the children, suffered from ignorance, filth, disease, the machinations of corrupt landlords and politicians, and not least, their own fear. Into this world stepped the sickly thirty-nine-year-old nun, with nothing but her own faith and the blessings of the pope to guide her. Her sense of doubt and fear must have been overwhelming, but as always in her life her determination was insurmountable." And so it was that within a few short months of her arrival in New York, Mother Cabrini established her orphanage, despite powerful opposition from several members of New York society and even the local church.

"Like Saint Teresa," Mother Cabrini often said, "with five pennies and God, I can accomplish many great things." Each time she set her heart on establishing a new institution, whether it was an orphanage, a hospital, or a convent, she seemed to find a way to finance it with little more than five pennies. Not long after establishing her orphanage in New York City, for example, she set her mind on obtaining a beautiful 450-acre estate on the

What are we to receive? A kingdom. For doing what? "I was hungry and you fed me." What is more ordinary, more of this world, than to feed the hungry, and yet it rates the Kingdom of Heaven.

—SAINT AUGUSTINE

Hudson River to provide her children with a more suitable environment for their growth. The estate was owned by a group of Jesuits who were willing to part with the property because they had tried several times to find water but had failed. Mother Cabrini told the Jesuits she would buy the estate, even though she had no idea where she would get the money. As she told her fellow sisters at the time, "The Jesuits are packing and going to another monastery they have built in Peekskill. I told them Our Lord is my banker and will not fail to help me find the money. These problems overcome my naturally weak condition and make me strong. The bigger the problem, the stronger I become. And now, I would like nothing better than a plate of rice à la Milanese and a glass of cool beer."

Mother Cabrini soon raised the money needed to buy the estate. She then prayed to Saint Mary to help her find water. The Blessed Mother appeared to her in a dream and told her where to dig the well. The following day she hired laborers and told them where to begin digging. They quickly unearthed a mountain spring that provided the orphanage with a continuous supply of fresh water.

One of the most striking instances of Mother Cabrini's uncanny ability to see her dreams come true occurred in Seattle in 1912, when she learned that one of her orphanages lay in the path of a planned highway expansion and would have to move. One night, after unsuccessfully searching the city on foot for a new location, Mother Cabrini had a dream of a villa on a hill. She tracked down the property she had seen in her dream and remarked calmly to her fellow sisters, "That paradise will be for our orphans, somehow or another."

As they headed back to their convent on foot from the villa, the nuns were exhausted. Mother Cabrini considered hiring a taxi, but she didn't want to spend the money. Just then a limousine with a single passenger happened to pass by, and Mother Cabrini hailed it. The female passenger offered to give the tired nuns a ride back to their convent. Along the way, Mother Cabrini began discussing her dream and the villa she had just seen.

The woman slowly realized that her passenger was the now-famous Mother Cabrini and that the property she was discussing was actually her own home.

"Mother Cabrini, the property you saw today, the 'paradise' you speak of—I own it. I had never thought of parting with it. But if I may be allowed to enter your holy house for just a moment and receive from your hands a glass of water in the name of Our Lord, your little orphans shall have their 'paradise' with all my heart." Mother Cabrini would later say that she acquired the property with three treasures: "my love, a dream, and a glass of water in His name."

Despite a desire to retire, to reflect and pray for the remaining days of her life, Mother Cabrini remained as head of her ever-growing order of missionary nuns, working tirelessly for the nation's poorest, until the day she died, on December 22, 1917. Upon her death, those who had known her or heard of her works began to pray for her intercession. Within ten years of her death, 150,000 reports of her favors were sent to the Pope from all parts of the world, urging him to make her a saint. In 1946, Mother Cabrini was canonized as a woman so endowed with the spirit of service that she dared to devote her life to others. Her courage, persistence, gentle humor, and undying compassion for those in need continue to inspire thousands to devote their lives to compassionate service in the name of God.

A PRAYER TO MOTHER FRANCES CABRINI

For Calmness and Kindness

Through your missionary work you radiated great light to those in need. Yours was a simple way, a kindly way, yet you accomplished many great and small tasks. I ask that you help me to stay calm and unwavering in the pursuit of my own projects of compassion. Mother Cabrini, bolster my faith in my many moments of doubt. Help me find the simple way.

Saint Frances Cabrini from a holy card.
(Maryknoll Fathers)

15

A HEART
OF CLOVER

Saint Patrick

A few years ago, on March 14 during a business trip to New Orleans, I struck up a conversation with a young couple from California on an airport shuttle van. Joyous, raucous, and unusually friendly, this young couple was delighted to be in New Orleans. "Why did you come to New Orleans?" I asked. "We're going to participate in the Saint Patrick's Day parade tomorrow," they said. "We've been looking forward to this for quite some time." There were about twelve of us on the van, and I soon learned that the majority of my co-travelers had also come to participate in the annual parade. Out of curiosity, I asked the group if anyone could tell me about the life of Saint Patrick. Why was he a saint, and why was his parade so important to them? Not a single person on the van had any idea who Saint Patrick really was, save that he was the patron saint of Ireland and had miraculously chased away the snakes from the island nation. As these acquaintances so readily proved, Saint Patrick is one of the most legend-shrouded figures in history.

To those familiar only with the mythic life of Saint Patrick, it will come as a surprise to learn that he was not a native Irishman but an Englishman. Born in 390 to a well-to-do Romanized Christian family, Saint Patrick studied both Latin and theology as a youth but

excelled at neither. As indifferent to his faith as he was to his studies, there was nothing about him that indicated future greatness. But sometime around his sixteenth birthday, in 403, he was forced to embark on a path of danger and discovery that would alter his life.

While the facts are somewhat sketchy, it appears that a band of Irish pirates came to Britain on a raid, seized young Patrick, took him back to Ireland, and turned him into a slave. He remained in slavery for the next six years, managing pigs for an Irish chieftain. In the loneliness of his captivity, Saint Patrick became fervently religious. As he would later write in his autobiographical *Confessions* (the only truly reliable information we have about his life), he roamed the hillsides of Ireland praying constantly to God. "Love and fear of God increased more and more in me. My faith grew and my spirit was stirred up, so that in a single day I said as many as a hundred prayers, and at night nearly as many. I used to stay in the woods and on the mountains. And before the dawn, I awakened to pray in snow, frost and rain; nor was there any lukewarmness in me such as I sometimes feel, so fervent was the Spirit within me."

One evening while he slept, just shortly before dawn, Saint Patrick was visited in his dreams by an angel. Frightened, he listened as the angel spoke: "Well do you fast and well do you pray. Soon you will see your own land again. Your ship is already waiting." Without delay he ran away from his master and walked nearly two hundred miles to an Irish seaport, where a group of sailors agreed to sail him to safety. After an additional twenty-eight-day journey over land, he was finally reunited with his family in Britain. He had been away from home for nearly six years.

After undergoing this physically exhausting and emotionally wrenching ordeal, Saint Patrick often found himself awakened at night by voices and visions of the Irish countryside. The voices implored him to return to Ireland to save the souls of the Irish. One night he had a particularly powerful dream that would transform his life. As he recounted in his *Confessions:* "I saw a man who seemed to be coming from Ireland. His name was Victo-

Saint Patrick
(Maryknoll Fathers)

rinus, and he was carrying an enormous number of letters. One of these he handed me, and I saw that it was headed 'The Voice of the Irish.' And as I began to read, I thought I could hear within me that same voice of the people who lived near the wood of Foclut, not far from the Western sea. And they called out as follows: 'We beseech you, holy youth, to come and walk once more among us.' I was so affected to the depths of my heart that I was unable to read further, and I awakened from my sleep."

Called by his visions to embark on a new and bolder life, Saint Patrick immediately set sail for France to study for Holy Orders under Saint Germanus of Auxerre. After completing his studies, he asked the Church to send him to Ireland, but instead of him they chose the first Irish bishop, Palladius. A year or two later, however, Palladius died. Pope Celestine I then sent Saint Patrick to Ireland to replace the deceased bishop.

Once in Ireland, Saint Patrick decided to concentrate his efforts on the western and northern portions of the country, where the Gospel had seldom if ever been preached. He worked vigorously to evangelize these regions, establishing many churches and monasteries, opening schools, and introducing the Irish to the Latin language.

Although he had a strong apocalyptic faith, Saint Patrick was never a hell-and-damnation preacher. He drew heavily upon the Bible for his sermons and throughout his writings stressed God's goodness, love, and care for those who sought Him. His piety was genuine, warm, and deep. Along with his simple message of love, his appreciation for Irish culture soon won over the Irish people. He never hesitated to give his converts control of their church structures; this enabled the Irish to establish their Christian faith on indigenous foundations. Saint Patrick allowed clergy to marry and presented monogamy as the Christian ideal. Perhaps more important, he never rushed the Irish. He allowed them the time they needed to absorb and assimilate Christianity with their own ancient customs.

Moved by Patrick's commitment and care for them, the Irish converted in large numbers. By the time of his death in 461, nearly the entire island

A brother asked Abba Poemen, "How should I behave in my cell in the place where I am living?" He replied, "Behave as if you were a stranger, and wherever you are, do not expect your words to have any influence and you will be at peace."
—THE DESERT FATHERS

had converted to Christianity. Never in the history of the Church has there been a more successful missionary. Through it all, Saint Patrick remained humble. "I, Patrick, a sinner, am the most ignorant and of least account among the faithful, despised by many. . . . I owe it to God's grace that so many people should through me be born again to Him."

Saint Patrick exhibited none of Saint Joan's heroic fireworks. None of Saint Jerome's fiery prose. None of Saint Augustine's dazzling intellect. Yet converts flocked to him because he converted by example. And there is a lesson in this for all of us, I suspect. Saint Patrick took the words "love your neighbor as yourself" seriously. Unlike so many of the missionaries who came before or after him, Saint Patrick managed to practice a rare form of unconditional love because he had divested himself almost entirely of his identification with his own culture.

Quite unlike the many Christian missionaries who were sent to Asia during the medieval period, Saint Patrick never regarded his native English culture as superior. Instead, he shared the emotions, thoughts, and feelings of his adopted people. Only then could the Irish see the true Christian message rather than the cultural wrappings that so often clothe the missionary. Saint Patrick never sought to change the Irish. All he did was try to love them in the name of God.

Saint Patrick was by no means a brilliant man, but he was a creative laborer who relied on the dictates of his heart when faced with a challenge. As a result there was never a barrier between Saint Patrick and his converts. He was a totally transparent, holy, and humble man. He reached out his hand to strangers with sincerity and love. That, I am sure, is the primary task of all men and women devoted to compassionate service.

A PRAYER
TO SAINT PATRICK

For Humility

You were an evangelical saint who came to love a people foreign to you with all your heart. Never once did you claim that your ways were superior to theirs or try to impose your will on others. I ask that you give me your ability to act toward others with sensitivity and care. Help me to learn to discern and share the emotions, thoughts, and feelings of my friends and loved ones, of strangers and adversaries, so that I can act toward them in a loving way. I ask that the wisdom you gained in reaching out to strangers with humility and love become the essence of my spiritual life.

16

THE INTERIOR CASTLE

———

Saint Teresa of Ávila

G od, deliver me from sullen saints," Teresa of Ávila often said. And God seems to have answered her prayers, for she was far from a sullen woman. Like Saint Francis and his friars, she carried laughter with her nearly everywhere she went, and she was just as happy to point it at herself as she was at her friends. She even poked fun at God on occasion: "No wonder You have so few friends when You treat the ones You have so badly." Teresa was undoubtedly a charmer and a great rarity in the history of sainthood, for she was at once a reformer, a mystic, and a comedian. Hers was a legacy of love, of contemplation-in-action, and for this reason she is universally admired.

Teresa's story begins, appropriately enough, with a smile. In 1522, as a seven-year-old living in the province of Old Castile, she apparently concocted a bold plan to run away with her brother. She ran away not to join the circus or to explore the marvels of a video arcade but to convert the Moors to Christianity. Fortunately, her uncle Francisco caught up with her outside the walls of Ávila and brought her home. Her only real disappointment in the episode was that she never had time to taste the dried raisins she had packed for what she believed would be her journey to martyrdom.

The Ecstasy of Saint Teresa.
(Bernini, Alinari Art Resource, NY)

Several religious biographers have used this story as evidence of Teresa's early calling to God, but I think it a better example of her inborn impulsiveness—her desire to make the bold move.

After this early quest for evangelism, what we know of Teresa's life was much like that of any other well-to-do young girl growing up in sixteenth-century Spain—or modern-day America, for that matter. Religious commitment was not her strong suit. By all accounts, she was an attractive girl who loved parties, romance novels, and flirting with the young Castilian men of Ávila. Only in her early twenties did she decide to enter a Carmelite convent, and her motivation to do so was inspired by a passion not to serve God but to remove herself from the temptations of worldly life. Quite simply, she feared she would go to hell if she did not moderate her behavior (not that it was ever so bad), and she saw the rigid life of the convent as a means of protecting herself. As she told a young man who was admiring her lovely dancing slippers a few days before she entered the convent, "Take a good look, sir. You won't be getting another chance." And she was right.

Teresa's father strongly protested her decision to enter the convent, and he refused to grant her his permission. But at twenty-one years of age, with the same boldness that would characterize her entire life, she stole away during the night and entered the Carmelite Convent of the Incarnation. The decision to leave her beloved father's house caused her great pain, but she felt she had no choice. "When I left my father's house, I felt the separation so keenly that the feeling will not be greater, I think, when I die. For it seemed that every bone in my body was being sundered," she wrote in her autobiography.

Less than a year into her life as a nun, Teresa fell gravely ill with what appears to have been either heart disease or palsy. Her grief-stricken father removed her from the convent and took her to her half-sister's house for treatment by a local healer. Despite the herbal treatments, her health did not improve. But it was during this time she obtained a copy of a book called _The Third Spiritual Alphabet,_ by Francisco de Osuna, a Franciscan

monk. This book is widely regarded as the first attempt in Spanish to describe the stages of contemplative prayer, and until she read it, Teresa confessed, she had had no idea how to pray inwardly. Her prayers had always been recited out loud and were rigorously structured.

Church officials at the time disapproved of the "mental prayer" described in Francisco de Osuna's book, fearing that it might lead people to think that all they had to do to gain access to the kingdom of God was to turn inward. Charity and penance would then become totally unnecessary. So the Church urged people to read such books with great caution. But Teresa was "delighted with the book and determined to follow its instructions with all [my] strength."

While Teresa's prayer life improved, her health deteriorated to the point that her heart felt as if "sharp teeth were being plunged into it." Her agony was so great that she could not sleep, so she left her half-sister's home and went to live with her father. By August, Teresa had passed into a deep coma, and her family feared she was dead, so they gave her Last Rites and dug her grave. For three days she lay motionless, but on the fourth day she managed to open her eyes—a task made quite difficult because wax had already been smeared over her eyes in preparation for her funeral. When she finally came to, Teresa found herself paralyzed, unable to move any but one of the fingers on her right hand. Despite her condition, she insisted on returning to the convent. Her paralysis would last another eight months, and it would be three years before she could leave her bed. "And when I started to crawl around on all fours, I praised God for it," she wrote. She attributed her recovery to the intercession of Saint Joseph, a saint she held in lifelong esteem.

In the years that followed, Teresa slowly regained her health, but for some reason she lost her ability to pray. This development troubled her more than her worst days of sickness. "I was more anxious that the hour I had determined to spend in prayer be over than I was to remain there . . . and so unbearable was the sadness I felt on entering the oratory, that

Saint Teresa of Ávila is the Patroness of Spain and is invoked against headaches and heart disease. She remains one of the world's most beloved mystics.
(Institute of Carmelite Studies, Washington, D.C.)

I had to muster up all my courage," she wrote in her autobiography, *The Book of Her Life*. She would spend the next eighteen years in this anguished, prayerless state.

The remarkable turning point in Saint Teresa's life came in 1555, at the age of forty, when she was given a copy of Saint Augustine's *Confessions*. "When I started reading the *Confessions* it seemed to me that I was seeing my own self right there," she would later recall. She broke down in tears, realizing that even those called to God often fall and must rise and repent again. The experience changed her entire religious life, for she began to pray once more.

Teresa entered upon her new life of prayer with great trepidation, owing to the fact that the tragic story of Magdalena de la Cruz of Cordoba was being widely circulated at the time. For as long as Teresa could recall, Magdalena had been regarded as a woman of extreme holiness, blessed with many miracles. But eight years earlier, Magdalena had confessed to the Inquisition that her miraculous works were nothing but the work of the Devil, with whom she had made a pact at the age of five. The Spanish nation had been scandalized by this news, and Teresa was haunted by the idea that she too could be led astray by the Devil through her practice of contemplative prayer. But she finally concluded that "the best thing I could do was to keep a clear conscience and avoid occasions even for venial sin. For if the spirit of God was behind it all, then the gain was clear; if it was the Devil, so long as I tried to please the Lord and keep from offending him, he could do me little harm and would rather be the loser."

Within a short period of time, mystical experiences were sweeping Teresa quite regularly. She dutifully sought the advice of several spiritual counselors to help her decipher her mystical insights. In 1559, when Teresa was forty-four, she had a powerful vision of the resurrected Christ. At this point, her confessor, Father Alvarez, advised her to resist any further visions. But Teresa was completely unable to heed his advice. "In these raptures it seems that the soul no longer animates the body, which thus loses

A very treacherous temptation is a feeling of security that we shall never relapse in to our former faults or care for worldly pleasures again.
—SAINT TERESA OF ÁVILA

its natural heat and gradually grows cold, though with a feeling of very great sweetness and delight. Here there is no way of resisting." Teresa's raptures became so powerful that, as she wrote, "Even at times my whole body has been lifted from the ground." She once asked her fellow nuns to help hold her down so that those listening to the mass sermon would not notice her levitation. "But it was noticed all the same," she recalled.

Despite the intensity of her mystical moments, Teresa's life at the convent was calm, pleasant, and predictable. But one day in 1560 she felt commanded by God to found a new order of Carmelites, rededicated to the austere rules of the founding fathers. Saint Teresa herself admitted that she undertook this project with some reluctance. "I was very happy in the house where I was. The place was much to my taste, and so was my cell, which suited me excellently." Nevertheless, she quietly began seeking allies for her project. Father Alvarez would not be one of them and encouraged her to drop her mission. Others cautioned her to tread lightly for fear of the Inquisition. But the more resistance she ran into, the more committed and courageous she became. This criticism "merely struck me as funny and made me laugh. On that score I never had any fear," she wrote.

Saint Teresa proposed to form entirely new communities in which the original ardor of the Carmelite tradition would be restored: rigorous fasting, many hours of daily prayer, modest clothing, and no bedding other than the ground and a stone for a pillow. By 1561, with the help of a lay patron, she had found a new home for her fledgling order. The following year, her new Carmelite convent, to be named Saint Joseph's, got papal approval. However, the more relaxed Calced Carmelites deeply resented Teresa's implication that their life was in need of reform. The unreformed Carmelite orders soon demanded outright suppression of Saint Teresa's new order. Despite their opposition, the next eight years of Saint Teresa's life were a time of incessant activity in which she founded seven convents. Yet this wasn't enough, for Teresa began to see that her reform efforts would flounder unless she expanded her mission to include men. It was at about this

Unless you are careful, praise from others may harm you greatly, for when once it begins it never ceases, and generally ends in running you down afterwards.

—SAINT TERESA OF ÁVILA

time that she was fortunate enough to meet Saint John of the Cross at Medina del Campo. He and a companion decided to join her reform movement as its first friars.

Saint Teresa took an instant liking to Saint John's humble, loving spirit, noting that "he was so good that I at least had more to learn from him than he from me." Together the pair undertook the reform of the Carmelite order. "Although we have had a few disagreements over business matters," Saint Teresa wrote of Saint John in a letter, "and I have sometimes been vexed with him, we have never seen the least imperfection in him." For his part, Saint John took advantage of his role as Saint Teresa's confessor to chide her gently. "When you make your confession, Mother, you have a way of finding the prettiest excuses." He tried to teach Saint Teresa about the "prayer of union," which he described as the complete renunciation of self to make room for God. For her part, she tried to write down her thoughts on mystical union for him, telling him that the moments of union she experienced were "gone in a flash." Their unusual friendship allowed Saint Teresa to trust completely—perhaps for the first time—the utter purity of her confessor. Together they forged a rare and lasting bond of friendship.

Within fifteen years of founding her order, at the age of sixty-seven, Saint Teresa suffered a severe stroke. Sensing that she had but a short time to live, she gathered her nuns together. "My daughters and ladies: For the love of God I beg you to observe most faithfully the Rule and the Constitutions. If you keep them as faithfully as you should, you will need no further miracle for your canonization. Do not imitate the poor example set you by this bad nun, but forgive me," she told those gathered on October 2, 1582. Two days later, she was dead.

Saint Teresa established seventeen convents and fourteen priories in her lifetime. Within six years of her passing, a papal order would establish the Discalced Carmelites as a fully independent order. Saint Teresa was canonized in 1622 and made a Doctor of the Church in 1970 for her many

books on mysticism, including her most famous, *The Mansions of the Interior Castle,* which tells of the soul's journey along the mystic way.

Saint Teresa believed that love is the essential feature of true mystical prayer, and that the flowering of love in every daily activity is the goal of spiritual life. She managed to wed contemplation with action almost flawlessly, for she was able to pass from the sublime to the everyday with the greatest ease of any saint in history. Perhaps because love and prayer were one and the same for her, love flowed over into every aspect of her life. As she wrote, "Love alone, however manifest, leads to union with God." For her, love led to mysticism, and mysticism to love. The true fruits of the contemplative life are seen in loving action, for love is the heart of prayer itself: "If you would progress a long way along this road, the important thing is not to think much, but to love much. Do then whatever arouses you to love." Better advice has seldom been offered.

A PRAYER
TO SAINT TERESA
OF ÁVILA

For Balance

You once prayed to God to "deliver me from sullen saints." Your life is a legacy of humor and love, action and contemplation. I ask that you help me to remember that life is best lived when viewed as an adventure in love. As you once said, "Love alone, however manifest, leads to union with God."

Saint Teresa being instructed by the Holy Spirit.

17

PASSAGE THROUGH THE NIGHT

Saint John of the Cross

Like few other saints, Saint John of the Cross (1542–1591) represents the blossoming of hope. For centuries, people have turned to his writings for solace and comfort, for this gentle mystic forever insisted that despair is as necessary to spiritual growth as mystical elation. In his many writings on spiritual life and particularly in his classic book, *The Dark Night of the Soul,* Saint John of the Cross insisted that great despair generally leads to great hope; that great hope eventually leads to great faith; and that great faith invariably leads to God. So long as there is hope, our faith will lead us to God. As Kenneth Leach says in his elegantly written book on spiritual direction, *Soul Friend,* "In hope, we wait in the dark, like watchmen awaiting the dawn."

Gail DeGeorge, a young woman in her thirties who holds down a demanding professional job in Miami, Florida, knew little about Saint John of the Cross's understanding of crisis. Her life had run quite smoothly for nearly thirty years, so she had never found the need to examine his writings. As she told me recently, "I never had reason to ever doubt the existence of God until my fiancé, Willie, was killed in an airplane crash in Africa." In the ensuing months of depression that clouded her life, Gail learned what it meant to have all

the props pulled out from under her, and what Saint John of the Cross meant when he described the "dark night of the soul."

Gail's darkest night came when she was spending an evening by herself rereading letters she had received from Willie during his many travels. As she sat alone with those letters, her thoughts turned to the many joyous times they had shared together. Overcome with a sense of loss and grief, she broke down and prayed to God for an answer as to why this wonderful man had been taken from her. Was her love lost? Would she ever regain her faith in the goodness of life?

After an evening of painful inner struggle, Gail awoke the following morning to find that two of the three roses she had purchased the day before were in glorious full bloom. The third rose, however, had wilted and died. As she told me, "That third rose was taller than the others, and when I purchased it, it represented Willie to me, because he was such a tall man. In the moment that I saw his rose lying there limp, I knew that God had given me a sign that love does indeed outlast death. Willie had died, but those other roses were blooming with splendor. Life goes on, and it is beautiful and good. It was still many months before I finally recovered, but at that moment I knew I was on the right track. My sense of hope had been reawakened, and I knew it was only a matter of time before I would be well again."

Like Saint John of the Cross, Gail's "dark night of the soul" eventually led to a flowering of hope and renewed faith. Her groping journey toward God was marked with pitfalls and failures, but today she has married and borne a son and says with utter confidence that "love outlasts death." She now appreciates the wisdom of Saint John, for she has come to agree with him that there is "a dark night through which the soul passes in order to attain the Divine light." Only by passing through a period of darkness, a time when one's faith seems as dry and arid as a desert, can we accept God for who and what He is, says Saint John.

. . .

For all that he wrote, Saint John is largely a mystery. He seems to have been self-reliant to the point of never really needing anyone in his life. Naturally drawn to solitude, he was a man of serene temperament who found most everyday events irrelevant to the search for God. "Worldly affairs take away the cloak of peace and the quiet of loving contemplation," he wrote in the *Spiritual Canticle*.

Yet because of his passion for God, Saint John of the Cross was to his friends that most valued of persons, a good listener. When he was asked to teach, he always did so with a selfless spirit, speaking little of himself or even of his listeners, but only of guiding the soul toward God by renouncing everything for Him. As he wrote in *The Ascent to Mount Carmel* (a treatise that was never finished), "That you may have pleasure in everything, seek pleasure in nothing. That you may know everything, seek to know nothing. That you may possess all things, seek to possess nothing. That you may be everything, be nothing."

Saint John's belief that we must ultimately give up our attachment to the things of this world to gain access to the Kingdom of God is obviously rooted in the New Testament. But his mature convictions can also be traced to his poverty-stricken upbringing. Born San Juan de la Cruz in Fontiveros in Spain in 1542, his father, Gonzalo de Yepes, came from a wealthy Toledan family of silk merchants. His mother, Catalina Alvarez, was reared by poor silk weavers. When Gonzalo married Catalina in 1529, his disapproving family disinherited him and forced the couple to resettle in the barrios of Fontiveros, a large village of some five thousand residents. There Gonzalo and Catalina made their home with the poorest of the poor.

In this environment of poverty and hardship, three sons were born to the struggling couple, but Gonzalo fell ill and died just after the birth of his third son, Juan (Saint John). Catalina was left utterly destitute, and within a few short years her second son, Louis, died from malnutrition.

Young Saint John barely survived himself and would never grow taller than five feet due to rickets. He would suffer from ill health his entire life.

For the poor families of sixteenth-century Spain, the only opportunity for education and advancement rested with the army or the Church. As Saint John was too small and too handicapped for military service, Catalina placed him in an orphanagelike catechism school, where he received religious and vocational instruction. The school arranged for Saint John's apprenticeship in carpentry and weaving, but he showed little promise in these crafts. Shy, thoughtful, and physically weak, it wasn't long before he recognized his future was not in the world of labor but in the universe of ideas. So from 1559 through 1563, he attended the newly established Jesuit college at Medina del Campo, where he received a classical education in the humanities.

Saint John did not find the Jesuit intellectual life to his liking, however, and slowly gravitated toward the contemplative orders of the Franciscans and Carmelites. In 1563 he entered a Carmelite monastery in Medina del Campo, becoming a friar at the age of twenty. Within a few short years he was ordained a priest and started what would become a lifelong friendship with Saint Teresa of Ávila, who was working at the time to form a new and far more rigorous Carmelite order.

Saint Teresa would later write of Saint John, "He was always a saint." She told him that God had called him to sanctify himself in her new order, and she asked him to consider leading one of the two new houses for men. Inspired, Saint John and his friend, Father Heredia, became the first two men to join Saint Teresa. Her efforts to found the new monasteries met with great opposition from a number of other powerful clergymen, however.

In 1577, the Provincial of Castile went so far as to order Saint John to return to his original friary at Medina del Campo. The gentle mystic refused, claiming that Saint Teresa's orders to found the new monasteries had come from a far higher authority, the papal nuncio in Rome. Appar-

Faith tells us of things we have never seen, and cannot come to know by our natural senses.

—SAINT JOHN OF THE CROSS

ently no one believed him, because on the night of December 2, 1577, a group of Carmelite monks and laymen pulled Saint John and his companion, German de San Matia, from their beds and pressed them to abandon their reforms. Upon Saint John's refusal, he was beaten and locked in a small, dark cell.

Taken captive by his own Carmelite brothers, Saint John was punished severely for his attempts to reform their order. For nine months he was imprisoned in Toledo in a cell so cold, he developed frostbite on his toes. Alban Butler writes in *Lives of the Saints* that the cell "measured ten feet by six, and the one window was so small and high up that he had to stand on a stool by it to see to read his office. He was bloodily beaten—he bore the marks to his dying day." His jailer was not allowed to talk with him or to remove waste from his cell, causing Saint John to fall ill from the stench. Often monks from the Calced order would stand outside his door and taunt him with news of a reformed convent that had been recently suppressed, all the while assuring Saint John that he would never be released.

After six months, Saint John's jailer was replaced by a far more tolerant and compassionate man, who gave him paper and a pen and allowed him to clean his cell. It was at this time that Saint John began to write the first "Spiritual Canticle," one of the most powerful mystical writings ever composed. In his dank cell, where he had felt such great emptiness and isolation, he entered into himself to find God, and came to see His presence in the wonders of the world:

> *My beloved mountains,*
> *The valley's solitary groves,*
> *The sounding rivers and fountains,*
> *The distant island's soil,*
> *The wind whistling love's song*
> *The calm night,*
> *The twin of the rising dawn,*

The silent music,
The sounding solitude,
The supper that kindles love and warms.

Yet Saint John was not content with the external beauty of the Divine Creation, for he knew—as all mystics know—that the beautiful world of the "Spiritual Canticle" must ultimately be left behind, for the Beloved is best met inside rather than outside. God is the flame, the reality behind the great beauty of our world, and we find Him at His purest in the center of our hearts. As Saint John wrote in "Love's Living Flame":

O Love's living flame,
Tenderly you wound
My soul's deepest center!
Since you no longer evade me,
Will you, please, at last conclude:
Rend the veil of this sweet encounter!

Within his cell, Saint John managed to find God in the center of his heart. But his isolation from the world of men would soon end, for his jailer had made a terrible mistake: He gave the mystic a needle and thread to mend his clothes. Instead, Saint John used them to stitch together his sheets to create a rope. At the same time, over a period of days, he slowly loosened the screws on the lock to his cell, until one night he was able to remove the lock from his cell door, fling his rope off the monastery's balcony, and descend into the garden below. Legend has it that Saint John was then led to a wall by a dog, climbed over it, and ran to a nearby Carmelite convent to hide. The nuns gave him shelter under the pretext that he was an extremely sick man in need of confession. Thus shielded, Saint John began to recover and continued working on his spiritual poems.

In the summer of 1588 the pope ratified a separation agreement between the reform and unreformed orders. The following year, Saint John became the prior of a tiny convent in Andalusia, El Calvario. Here he wrote *The Dark Night of the Soul,* in which he described those moments when God seems absent from the soul; "it finds no consolation or support in any instruction nor in any spiritual master."

After the death of Saint Teresa in 1582, disagreements arose among the members of her new order. Saint John believed that the religious vocation was contemplative in nature and that members should not leave their houses or monasteries to preach. But many did not agree with him. Saint John's most vocal opponent was Father Nicholas Doria, who had been prior of El Calvario before Saint John replaced him. In an effort to halt the squabbling between them, Saint John agreed to allow Doria to strip him of his offices. Saint John was then sent to the remote friary of La Penvela, where he became a marginal man in the Carmelite order.

Saint John was ill treated and humiliated at La Penvela. His health worsened to the point that he had to be moved to a small, secluded priory in Ubedam. The superior there, Francisco Crisostomo, treated him with great severity because he disdained the fact that a few Carmelites viewed John as a living saint. Even as his health plummeted, Crisostomo denied Saint John the food prescribed by his doctor, alleging that the monastery was too poor to do as the doctor ordered. Finally, on December 14, 1591, after suffering horribly for three months, Saint John asked to be read "The Song of Songs." Suddenly he exclaimed: "Oh, what beautiful daisies!" and died.

Saint John died alone, with few admirers. Only a handful of nuns and a few novices recognized in his gentility and sincerity the traits of a saintly man. Yet the greatest of his works, *The Dark Night of the Soul, Spiritual Canticle,* and *Love's Living Flame,* continue to be read today as textbooks by students of mysticism. Saint John himself managed to condense

Saint John of the Cross shown hearing the word of God.
(Institute of Carmelite Studies, Washington, D.C.)

A PRAYER TO
JOHN OF THE CROSS

For Inspiration and Wonder

Poet, reformer, and gentle adventurer of the soul, you descended into the dark night and emerged transcendent. Your writings outline the steps of the mystic path and teach of the beauty that resides at the center of our hearts. I am forever grateful to you for this wisdom. I pray that you help me to find the mystic buried deep within me. Help me to understand the wonders of heaven and earth and to feel our basic oneness with these wonders.

the wisdom of his life into a five-step process, comparing the spiritual quest to the flight of a bird. The first step is "that it flies to the highest point; the second, that it does not suffer for company, nor even of its own kind; the third, that it aims its beak to the skies; the fourth, that it does not have a definite color; the fifth, that it sings very softly." The flight of Saint John was all of this and more.

EPILOGUE

—◆—

Three weeks after completing this book, on June 8, 1993, I went into labor with my second child, a girl my husband and I named Channa, which means "grace" in Hebrew. We had been expecting the labor to start any day, so when the first contractions came at 12:30 in the afternoon, I greeted them with excitement. As any mother knows, pain is relatively easy to bear so long as we remember how essential it is for the fulfillment of something wondrous.

But I would soon be faced with a far different sort of pain, a dreaded and wholly unexpected pain, because something went terribly wrong in the doctor's office. Channa's heartbeat began to slow and I was rushed to the hospital in a screaming ambulance. When I arrived they hurried me to the operating table, put me to sleep, and performed an emergency cesarean section. When I awoke some two hours later, groggy, exhausted, and scared, I was told that Channa had died. Her umbilical cord had crimped in my womb shortly after I went into labor and her tiny heart just couldn't stand the stress.

I had spent the previous nine months working on this book full-time as an act of prayer and hope, almost as an offering, confident that God would grant me a

healthy baby in return. I never wondered—as I do so often today—why I felt I had to make such a secret pact with God. After all, I was a decent person trying to convey in words what I thought it meant to live a spiritual life of humility, devotion, and gratitude. I didn't deserve to have a child die.

Many of my hours these past three months have been spent second-guessing the entire pregnancy. What did I do wrong? What if I had gone to the doctor's office in the morning? Why didn't we induce labor a few days earlier, as we had discussed? If I have learned anything at all about tragedies of this sort, it is that they present endless opportunities for second-guessing oneself. But I see now that "What if?" and "Why?" are not especially helpful questions for those who hurt. Suffering people are not at all concerned with "interesting questions" but with elemental ones.

Three months have passed since Channa died. And not a day has gone by when I have not thought of her and expressed my love to her, hoping that she knows she was loved by her mother and father. And not a day has gone by when I have not struggled with the unfairness of her death, and questioned if I ever had any spiritual comprehension of life and its mysteries. I have not lost my faith in God, but I have struggled to maintain faith in my spiritual vision. Yet for all my doubts and cries, I continue to believe with Saint Isaac of Syria that "God alone is the spring of love whose supply never fails."

No, the question is not why do tragedies occur, but how do we respond to them? As we all soon learn, life is full of good and wondrous things, but it is also punctuated by many bad things and, occasionally, a few horrible things. Each day, it seems, we are bombarded by the truth that life is neither easy nor fair and is often quite sick. As the saints have taught me, spiritual life is essentially about rising above this sickness; about finding a way to make sense of the many tragedies we observe and experience so that we can move forward with a greater sense of compassion and respect for all of God's creatures. Looking back over the lives of the saints I've studied,

Saint Ramon Nonnatus was delivered by cesarean section after his mother died in childbirth. Because of his difficult birth, he is invoked by women in labor and is the patron saint of midwives.
(Denver Art Museum)

there is one constant theme: an unwavering love for God and the desire to lift up his creation with all one's heart and soul. Tragedies and setbacks never seemed to deter the will of Mother Cabrini, Saint Joan, Saint Kolbe, or any number of other courageous men and women. A commitment to serving God by serving the needs of His creation drove them forward even under the most desperate of circumstances. Just as God's relentless compassion pursued the saints when they were at their worst, the saint's relentless compassion pursued the most desperate among the suffering.

As so many of the saints have stressed, we cannot grow into truly spiritual people without suffering, not simply because we cannot escape it, but because without it we cannot comprehend the meaning of love or the majesty of God's beauty. Not until I held my silent baby daughter in my arms did I come to understand the truth of something Kahlil Gibran once wrote: "Love knows not its own depth until the hour of separation." Why we must suffer so much to learn the ultimate lesson of gratitude for life remains a mystery to me. All I know is that it is true: Suffering is the teacher, love the lesson. For all the sadness I presently feel, I realize how much Channa's death has already taught me. I understand, for example, as I have never before, the many photos we have all seen of mothers hunched against the Wailing Wall in Jerusalem, weeping over the loss of a loved one. Before Channa's death I reacted to these photos with sympathy, but never truly understood the kind of pain that drives such uncontrollable anguish. Hours after holding Channa for the first and last time, however, I thought of these women, so often immortalized in photo and film, and finally understood what it meant to wail in pain. For there are times in life when suffering overwhelms us to the point that we can only wail. Yet this is not in vain, for the salty water of our tears is essential for inner growth; a more caring and compassionate heart reaches upward and outward, almost invariably, like the underappreciated crocuses that sprout up through our lawns in spring.

After she lost her husband and two of her daughters to tuberculosis,

Mother Seton had many opportunities to sink into depression. Yet she, like so many others whom life has hurt, was able to cultivate a compassionate life from the roots of her suffering. This is my hope as well. If I had a choice, I would do almost anything to have my daughter back and nursing at my breast today. But such a choice is not within my power. I am left only with today and tomorrow. So the great question of the saints remains: How should I live the rest of my life?

A few days ago, in an effort to lift my spirits from an emotional slump, I turned my thoughts to Saint Francis. I found myself marveling at his life and realized, as never before, how much brute strength and courageous determination it takes to be happy. Saint Francis reminded me that sometimes it takes more courage to turn to God than it does to turn away from Him. The start of any truly spiritual recovery must always begin with God, for all love begins with "Him who loved us into existence." As Robert Llewelyn wrote in *The Joy of the Saints,* "It is this all-embracing love of God, shed abroad in their hearts—strong and true, compassionate and enduring—which is the mark of the love of the saints."

So it is that I have returned to the beginning of my story. I was compelled to write this book in an effort to make sense of my brother's death some three years ago, and today I am faced with making sense of my daughter's death. The only difference between now and then is that I have spent the past few years studying the lives of the most courageous and spiritually gifted men and women who have ever lived. Today I am surrounded by spiritual comrades and teachers, guideposts on the way, many of whom have navigated successfully through far more treacherous and troubling waters than I have yet encountered. Have I found the answer? No, I have not, but I'm getting closer, and for this I have the saints to thank. Even now, as I mourn Channa's death, I can still hear the warm voice of Saint John of the Cross whisper in my ear: "Pour in love where there is no love, and you will draw out love." That may be as close to the truth as I will ever get. Now all I must do is strive to live it.

APPENDIX

Patron Saint Index

This extensive index is the product of long established customs and devotions designated to certain saints as patrons and protectors for those in certain professions or occupations as well as those which can be invoked in times of special need.

ABANDONED CHILDREN: St. Jerome Emiliani
ACCOUNTANTS: St. Matthew
ACTORS: St. Genesius
ADVERTISING: St. Bernardine
ALPINISTS: St. Bernard
ALTAR SERVERS: St. John Berchmans
AMERICA: Mary, Immaculate Conception
AMMUNITION WORKERS: St. Barbara
AMPUTEES: St. Anthony
ANESTHESIOLOGISTS: St. Rene
ANIMALS: St. Francis of Assisi
APOSTLESHIP OF PRAYER: St. Francis Xavier
APOTHECARIES: St. Raphael
APPLE ORCHARDS: St. Charles Borromeo
ARCHAEOLOGISTS: St. Helen
ARCHERS: St. Sebastian
ARCHITECTS: St. Barbara
ARGENTINA: Our Lady of Luzon
ARMENIA: St. Gregory Illuminator
ARMORERS: St. Sebastian
ARROWSMITHS: St. Sebastian

ART DEALERS: St. John the Evangelist
ARTHRITIS: St. James
ARTILLERY: St. Barbara
ARTISTS: St.Luke
ASIA MINOR: St. John the Evangelist
ASTRONOMERS: St. Dominic
ATHLETES: St. Sebastian
AUSTRALIA: St. Francis Xavier
AUSTRIA: St. Colman, St. Stephen
AUTHORS: St. Paul, Apostle; St. Francis de Sales
AVIATORS: St. Joseph Cupertino, St. Theresa, Our Lady
    of Loretto

BACHELORS: St. Christopher
BAKERS: St. Nicholas, St. Meingold
BANKERS: St. Matthew
BARBERS: Sts. Cosmas and Damian
BARREN WOMEN: St. Felicitas, St. Anthony
BASKET MAKERS: St. Anthony, Abbot
BATTLE: St. Michael
BEEKEEPERS: St. Ambrose
BEGGARS: St. Alexis
BELGIUM: St. Joseph
BELL FOUNDERS: St. Agatha
BELT MAKERS: St. Alexis
BIRDS: St. Francis of Assisi
BLACK CATHOLIC MISSIONS: St. Peter Claver
BLACKS: St. Martin de Porres
BLACKSMITHS: St. James
BLINDNESS: St. Odillia, St. Lawrence the Illuminator
BOATMEN: St. Julian Hospitallar
BODILY ILLS: Our Lady of Lourdes
BOHEMIA: St. Wenceslaus
BOOKBINDERS: St. Peter Celestine, St. Sebastian

BOOKKEEPERS: St. Matthew
BOOK SELLERS: Sts. John of God, John Evangelist
BORNEO: St. Francis Xavier
BOY SCOUTS: St. George
BRASS WORKERS: St. Barbara
BRAZIL: St. Peter of Alcantara, Immaculate Conception
BREWERS: St. Nicholas
BRIDES: St. Dorothy
BRIDGE BUILDERS: St. Peter
BRUISES: St. Amalberga
BRUSH MAKERS: St. Anthony, Abbot
BUILDERS: St. Vincent Ferrer, St. Barbara
BUTCHERS: St. Hadrian, St. Anthony, Abbot

CAB DRIVERS: St. Fiacre
CABINET MAKERS: St. Anne
CANADA: St. Anne, St. Joseph
CANCER: St. Peregrine, James Salamoni
CARPENTERS: St. Joseph
CASKET MAKERS: St. Stephen
CATECHISTS: St. Robert Bellarmine, St. Charles
    Borromeo
CATHOLIC ACTION: St. Francis of Assisi
CATHOLIC UNIVERSITIES: St. Thomas Aquinas
CATTLE DISEASES: St. Sebastian
CAVALRY: St. George
CEMETERY WORKERS: St. Anthony
CHARITY: St. Vincent de Paul
CHASTITY: St. Agnes
CHEMICAL INDUSTRIES: Sts. Cosmas and Damian
CHILDREN: St. Nicholas
CHILE: St. James, Our Lady of Mt. Carmel
CHINA: St. Francis Xavier, St. Joseph
CHOIR BOYS: Holy Innocents, St. Dominic Savio

CIVIL SERVANTS: St. Thomas More
CLERGY: St. Charles Borromeo
CLERICS: St. Gabriel of the Sorrowful Mother
CLOCK MAKERS: St. Peter
CLOTH DYEING: St. Lydia
CLOTHING INDUSTRY: St. Paul the Hermit
COLIC: St. Charles Borromeo
COLOMBIA: St. Peter Claver
COMEDIANS: St. Genesius
COMMUNICATIONS MEDIA: St. Gabriel the Archangel
COMPOSERS: St. Cecilia
COMPOSITORS: St. John the Evangelist
CONFECTIONERS: St. Joseph
CONFESSORS: St. Francis de Sales
CONVERSION AND BAPTISM: St. John the Baptist
CONVULSIONS IN CHILDREN: St. Scholastica
COOKS: St. Martha, St. Lawrence
COOPERS: St. Nicholas
COPPERSMITHS: St. Maurus
COUNSEL: Holy Spirit
COURT WORKERS: St. Thomas More
CRAMPS: St. Maurice
CZECHOSLOVAKIA: St. John Nepomucene, St. Wenceslaus

DAIRY WORKERS: St. Brigid
DANCERS: St. Genesius
DEAF: St. Francis de Sales
DENMARK: St. Ansgar
DENTISTS: St. Appolonia
DESPERATE SITUATIONS: St. Rita, St. Jude
DIABOLICAL POSSESSION: St. Bruno
DIETICIANS: St. Martha
DOCTORS: St. Luke

DOG BITES: St. Hubert
DOG FANCIERS: St. Roque
DOMESTIC ANIMALS: St. Anthony
DOMESTIC SERVANTS: St. Martha, St. Zita
DOUBT: St. Joseph
DRUGGISTS: St. Raphael the Archangel, Sts. Cosmas and Damian
DYING: St. Joseph

EAST INDIES: St. Thomas, Apostle
ECUADOR: Sacred Heart
EDITORS: St. John Bosco
EMIGRANTS: St. Frances Xavier Cabrini
ENEMIES OF RELIGION: St. Sebastian
ENGINEERS: St. Ferdinand, St. Joseph
ENGLAND: St. George
ENGRAVERS: St. John the Evangelist
ENLIGHTENMENT: Our Lady of Good Counsel
EPILEPSY: St. Genesius
ETHIOPIA: St. Frumentius
EXPECTANT MOTHERS: St. Elizabeth, St. Gerard
EYE DISEASES: St. Raphael the Archangel
EYES: St. Lucy

FAITH IN THE BLESSED SACRAMENT: St. Anthony
FALSELY ACCUSED: St. Raymond Nonnatus, St. Gerard
FAMILIES: St. Joseph
FAMILY HARMONY: St. Dymphna
FARMERS: St. Isidore
FEAR OF THE LORD: Holy Spirit
FEVER: St. Peter
FINLAND: St. Henry of Upsala
FIRE: St. Francis of Assisi

FIREMEN: St. Florian
FIRE PREVENTION: St. Catherine of Siena
FIREWORKS: St. Barbara
FIRST COMMUNICANTS: St. Tarcisius, St. Imelda, St.
    Pius X
FISHERMEN: St. Andrew, St. Peter
FLOODS: St. Columban
FLORISTS: St. Dorothy
FLOUR INDUSTRY WORKERS: St. Arnulph
FLYERS: St. Joseph Cupertino, Our Lady of Loretto
FOOT TROUBLE: St. Peter
FORTIFICATIONS: St. Barbara
FORTITUDE: Holy Spirit
FOUNDLINGS: Holy Innocents
FRANCE: St. Joan of Arc
FRENZY: St. Peter
FULLERS: St. James the Less
FUNERAL DIRECTORS: St. Dismas

GALLSTONES: St. Liberius
GAMBLING, UNCONTROLLED: St. Bernardine,
    St. Cajètan
GARDENERS: St. Dorothy, St. Sebastian
GERMANY: St. Boniface, St. Michael
GIRL SCOUTS: St. Agnes
GLANDULAR DISORDERS: St. Cadoc
GLASS INDUSTRY: St. Luke
GLAZIERS: St. Mark
GOLDSMITHS: St. Anastasius, St. Luke
GOUT: St. Andrew
GRANDMOTHERS: St. Anne
GRAVE DIGGERS: St. Anthony

*Saint Dorothy was tortured and beheaded on account of
her faith. As she was being led off to be beheaded a
man asked her scornfully for one of the roses she
claimed to have gathered at one time in the garden of
Jesus. Although it was winter, as Dorothy rested her
head on the block a child appeared with a basket of
roses and offered them to the scornful man. He
immediately converted and was later killed for his faith
as well.*

(Francesco di Giorgio, National Gallery of Art, London)

Saint Cajetan with Christ Child: In New Mexico, Saint Cajetan is considered the patron saint of gamblers. During his lifetime, he established homes for clergy and laity for the service of the sick and poor in Rome, Vicenza, and Venice.

(Denver Art Museum)

GREECE: St. Nicholas
GREETING CARDS INDUSTRY: St. Valentine
GROCERS: St. Michael
GUNNERS: St. Barbara

HAPPY DEATH: St. Joseph
HARDWARE: St. Sebastian
HATTERS: St. James the Less, St. Severus
HEADACHES: St. Denis
HEALING OF WOUNDS: St. Rita
HEART AILMENTS: St. John of God
HERNIA: St. Conrad
HESITATION: St. Joseph
HOLLAND: St. Willibrord
HOME BUILDERS: Our Lady of Loretto
HOPELESS CASES: St. Jude
HORSEMEN: St. Anne
HOSPITAL WORKERS: St. Vincent de Paul
HOSPITALS: St. Camillus, St. John of God, St. Vincent de Paul
HOTEL INDUSTRY WORKERS: St. Amandus
HOUSEKEEPERS: St. Martha, St. Anne
HOUSEWIVES: St. Anne
HUNGARY: St. Stephen of Hungary, Our Lady
HUNTERS: St. Eustace, St. Hubert

IMMIGRANTS: St. Frances Xavier Cabrini
IMPENITENCE: St. Barbara
IMPULSIVE GAMBLING: St. Bernardine
INFANTRYMEN: St. Maurice
INNKEEPERS: St. Julian the Hospitaller, St. Armand
INSANITY: St. Dymphna

INVALIDS: St. Roque
IRELAND: St. Columba, St. Patrick
IRON MONGERS: St. Sebastian
ITALY: St. Catherine of Siena

JAPAN: St. Peter Baptist
JESUIT ORDER: St. Ignatius of Loyola
JEWELLERS: St. Eligius
JOURNALISTS: St. Paul, Apostle; St. Francis de Sales
JUDGES: St. Ives
JURORS: St. Catherine of Alexandria

KNIGHTS: St. Michael
KNOWLEDGE: Holy Spirit

LABORERS: St. James
LACE MAKERS: St. Francis of Assisi
LAMP MAKERS: Our Lady of Loretto
LAST SACRAMENTS: St. Stanislaus
LATIN AMERICA: St. Rose of Lima
LAWYERS: St. Thomas More, St. Ives
LEAD WORKERS: St. Sebastian
LEARNING: St. Margaret of Scotland, St. Ambrose
LEPERS: St. Vincent de Paul
LIBERAL ARTS: St. Catherine of Bologna
LIBRARIANS: St. Jerome
LIGHTNING: St. Barbara
LITHOGRAPHERS: St. John the Evangelist
LITHUANIA: St. Casimir
LOCKSMITHS: St. Dunstan
LONELINESS: St. Rita

LONG LIFE: St. Peter
LOST ARTICLES: St. Anthony
LOVERS: St. Raphael
LUMBAGO: St. Lawrence
LUNATICS: St. Dymphna
LUNGS AND CHEST: St. Bernardine

MACHINISTS: St. Hubert
MAIDS: St. Zita
MALL SERVERS: St. John Berchmans
MANUAL LABORERS: St. James the Greater
MARBLE WORKERS: St. Clement I
MARINERS: St. Michael
MARRIED COUPLES: St. Joseph
MASONS: St. Peter
MASS MEDIA: St. Gabriel the Archangel
MATHEMATICIANS: St. Hubert
MEDICAL SOCIAL WORKERS: St. John Regis
MEDICAL TECHNOLOGISTS: St. Albert
MENTAL ILLNESS: St. Dymphna
MERCHANTS: St. Armand, St. Francis of Assisi
MESSENGERS: St. Gabriel the Archangel
METAL WORKERS: St. Hubert
MEXICO: Our Lady of Guadalupe
MILLERS: St. Arnulph
MINERS: St. Piron, St. Barbara
MISSIONERS: St. Francis Xavier
MISSIONS: St. Teresa, St. Francis Xavier
MONASTICS: St. Benedict
MONKS: St. Benedict
MORTICIANS: St. Joseph of Arimathea
MOTHERS: St. Gerard, St. Anne
MOTORCYCLISTS: Our Lady of the Miraculous Medal

MOTORISTS: St. Christopher
MOUNTAIN CLIMBERS: St. Bernard
MUSICIANS: St. Cecilia

NAIL MAKERS: St. Claude
NAVIGATORS: Our Lady, Star of the Sea
NEEDLE WORKERS: St. Francis of Assisi
NERVES: St. Dymphna
NET MAKERS: St. Peter
NEW ZEALAND: St. Francis Xavier
NEWBORN BABIES: St. Brigid
NORWAY: St. Olaf
NOTARIES: St. Luke, St. Ives
NUNS: St. Brigid
NURSES: St. Raphael, St. John of God, St. Camillus de
   Lellis

OBSTETRICIANS: St. Ramon Nonnatus
OLD MAIDS: St. Andrew
ORATORS: St. John Chrysostom
ORGAN MAKERS: St. Cecilia
ORPHANS: St. Jerome Emiliani, St. Louise

PAINTERS: St. Luke
PAPER MAKERS: St. John the Evangelist
PARATROOPERS: St. Michael
PARISH PRIESTS: St. John Vianney
PRINTERS: St. John the Evangelist
PRISONS: St. Joseph Cafasso
PRISONERS: St. Barbara, St. Vincent de Paul

PUBLIC RELATIONS: St. Bernardine
PUBLISHERS: St. Paul, Apostle; St. John the Evangelist

RACQUET MAKERS: St. Sebastian
RADIO WORKERS: St. Gabriel
RADIOLOGISTS: St. Michael
RAIN: St. Scholastica
RANCHERS: St. Isidore
REFUGEES: St. Alban
RETREATS: St. Ignatius of Loyola
RHEUMATISM: St. James the Greater
RUSSIA: St. Boris, St. Nicholas, St. Andrew

SADDLERS: St. Lucy
SAFE JOURNEY: St. Raphael
SAILORS: St. Brendan, Our Lady Star of the Sea, St.
   Michael, St. Cuthbert
SALESMEN: St. Lucy
SCHOLARS: St. Thomas Aquinas
SCHOOLS: St. Thomas Aquinas
SCIENTISTS: St. Albert
SCOTLAND: St. Andrew
SCRIBES: St. Catherine
SCULPTORS: St. Claude, St. Luke
SEAFARERS: St. Michael
SECRETARIES: St. Catherine
SEMINARIANS: St. Charles Borromeo
SERVANTS: St. Martha
SERVICE WOMEN: St. Joan of Arc
SHEEP RAISERS: St. Raphael
SHIP BUILDERS: St. Peter
SHOEMAKERS: St. Crispin

SICILY: St. Nicholas

SICK: St. Camillus de Lellis

SILVERSMITHS: St. Andronicus

SINGERS: St. Gregory the Great, St. Cecilia

SKATERS: St. Lidwina

SKIERS: St. Bernard

SKIN DISEASES: St. Roch, St. Peregrine

SNAKEBITE: St. Patrick

SOLDIERS: St. Sebastian, St. Ignatius of Loyola, St. George

SOLITARY DEATH: St. Francis of Assisi

SOUTH AMERICA: St. Rose of Lima

SPAIN: St. James the Great

SPELEOLOGISTS: St. Benedict

SPINSTERS: St. Catherine

SPIRITUAL DIRECTORS: St. Charles Borromeo

SPIRITUAL HELP: St. Vincent de Paul

SRI LANKA: St. Lawrence

STAINED GLASS WORKERS: St. Mark

STATIONERS: St. Peter

STENOGRAPHERS: St. Catherine

STOCKBROKERS: St. Matthew

STOMACH TROUBLE: St. Charles Borromeo

STONE MASONS: St. Barbara, St. Stephen, St. Sebastian

STONECUTTERS: St. Clement I

STONEWORKERS: St. Stephen

STORMS: St. Theodore, St. Barbara

STUDENTS: St. Thomas Aquinas

SUDDEN DEATH: St. Barbara

SURGEONS: Sts. Cosmas and Damian, St. Luke

SWEDEN: St. Brigit

SWITZERLAND: St. Antiochus, St. Nicholas

SWORDSMITHS: St. Dunstan, St. Maurice

TAILORS: St. Homobonus, St. John the Baptist

TANNERS: St. Simon Stock, St. James

TAXMEN: St. Matthew

TEACHERS: St. Gregory, St. Francis de Sales, St. Catherine of Alexandria, St. John Baptist de la Salle

TELEGRAPH: St. Gabriel

TELEPHONE WORKERS: St. Gabriel

TELEVISION: St. Clare of Assisi

TEMPTATION: St. Michael

TERTIARIES: St. Elizabeth of Hungary, St. Louis X

THEOLOGIANS: St. Augustine, St. Thomas Aquinas

THROAT: St. Blase

TINSMITHS: St. Joseph of Arimathea

TONGUE: St. Catherine

TOOTHACHE: St. Apollonia

TOY MAKERS: St. Claude

TRAVEL: St. Paul, Apostle; St. Christopher

TRUCK DRIVERS: St. Christopher

TUBERCULOSIS: St. Theresa of Lisieux

TUMORS: St. Rita

ULCERS: St. Charles Borromeo

UNCONTROLLED GAMBLING: St. Bernardine

UNDERSTANDING: Holy Spirit

UNDERTAKERS: St. Sebastian

UNITED STATES: Immaculate Conception

UNIVERSAL CHURCH: St. Joseph

VANITY: St. Rose of Lima

VETERINARIANS: St. James

VIRGINS: St. Agnes, St. Joan of Arc, the Virgin Mary

Saint Barbara was the beautiful daughter of a jealous man who locked her up to prevent her from seeing suitors. While imprisoned, she converted to Christianity. This enraged her father who beheaded her and was immediately struck down by lightning. Saint Barbara is invoked for protection from thunderstorms.
(Denver Art Museum)

VOCALISTS: St. Cecilia
VOCATIONS: St. Alphonsus

"WAC": St. Joan of Arc
"WAVES": St. Joan of Arc
WALES: St. David
WAREHOUSES: St. Barbara
WATCHMEN: St. Peter of Alcantara
WEAVERS: St. Anastasia, St. Bernabas
WEST INDIES: St. Gertrude
WHEELWRIGHTS: St. Catherine of Alexandria
WIDOWS: St. Louise
WILD ANIMALS: St. Blase
WINEMAKERS: St. Francis Xavier
WISDOM: Holy Spirit
WOLVES: St. Peter
WOMEN IN LABOR: St. Anne
WOOLWORKERS: St. Bernardine
WRITERS: St. Paul, Apostle; St. John the Evangelist

YACHTSMEN: Our Lady Star of the Sea
YOUTH: St. Aloysius Gonzaga, St. Gabriel of the
Sorrowful Mother, St. John Berchmans, St. Dominic
Savio, St. Maria Goretti

Meanings of Famous Saints' Names

Agatha (good)
Agnes (pure one)
Albert (noble; brilliant)
Ambrose (divine; immortal)
Andrew (strong; manly)
Angela (angel; messenger)
Ann (graceful one)
Anne (gracious one)
Anthony (inestimable)
Barbara (stranger)
Basil (kingly)
Benedict (blessed)
Bernadette (brave as a bear)
Catherine (pure one)
Cecilia (blind)
Charles (strong; manly)
Christine (Christian)
Christopher (Christ-bearer)
Clara (brilliant; bright)
Claudia (lame one)
Colette (victorious army)
Conrad (able in counsel)
Constance (firmness)
Cornelius (battle horn)
David (beloved one)
Dominic (belonging to God)
Dorothy (gift of God)
Edith (rich gift)
Edward (prosperous guardian)
Elizabeth (consecrated to God)

Emily (industrious)
Emma (nurse)
Eric (ever powerful)
Ferdinand (world-daring)
Frances (free one)
Francis (free one)
Frederick (peaceful)
Gabriel (man of God)
George (land worker)
Gerard (spear-brave)
Gertrude (spear-strength)
Gilbert (brilliant pledge)
Giles (shield-bearer)
Gregory (watchman)
Helen (light; torch)
Henry (ruler of estate)
Hilda (battle-maid)
Howard (chief; guardian)
Hubert (bright mind)
Isabel (consecrated to God)
James (supplanter)
Jerome (sacred name)
Joan (God is gracious)
John (God is gracious)
Joseph (He shall add)
Julia (youthful one)
Justin (just)
Katherine (pure one)
Kevin (gentle; lovable)
Lawrence (laurel-crowned one)

Leo (lion)
Louis (famous warrior)
Lucy (bringer of light)
Luke (bringer of light)
Maria (myrrh)
Marie (myrrh)
Mark (warlike one)
Martin (warlike one)
Mary (myrrh)
Matthew (gift of God)
Michael (who is like God)
Monica (advise)
Nicholas (victory of the people)
Patrick (noble one)
Paul (little)
Peter (rock)
Philip (lover of horses)
Priscilla (ancient birth)
Richard (powerful ruler)
Rita (a pearl)
Robert (shining with fame)
Rose (a rose)
Sophia (wisdom)
Stephen (crowned one)
Theresa (reaper)
Thomas (a twin)
Timothy (honoring God)
Veronica (true image)

Honorific Titles for Saints

Angel of the Schools: St. Thomas Aquinas (1225–74)
Angelic Doctor: St. Thomas Aquinas
Apostle of the Gauls: St. Denis (d.c. 258)
Apostle of Germany: St. Boniface (680–754)
Athanasius of the West: St. Hilary of Poitiers (c. 315–68)
Beloved Disciple: St. John the Evangelist (c. 6–104)
Beloved Physician: St. Luke the Evangelist (first century)
Bishop of Hippo: St. Augustine (354–430)
Christian Demosthenes: St. Gregory of Nazianzen (c. 329–89)
Divine Doctor: John Ruysbroeck (1293–1381)
Doctor Angelicus: St. Thomas Aquinas
Doctor Expertus: St. Albert the Great (c. 1206–80)
Doctor of Grace: St. Augustine
Doctor of Mystical Theology: St. John of the Cross (1542–91)
Doctor Universalis: St. Albert the Great
Dumb Ox: St. Thomas Aquinas
Eagle of Divines: St. Thomas Aquinas
Ecstatic Doctor: St. John Ruysbroeck
Evangelical Doctor: St. Anthony of Padua (1195–1231)
Father of Biblical Science: St. Jerome (c. 342–420)
Father of Church History: St. Eusebius (c. 283–371)
Father of Eastern Monasticism: St. Basil the Great (329–79)
Father of English History: Bede the Venerable (c. 672–735)
Father of Moral Philosophy: St. Thomas Aquinas
Father of Orthodoxy: St. Athanasius (c. 297–373)
Father of Scholasticism: St. Anselm (1036–86)
Golden-Tongued Orator: St. John Chrysostom (347–407)
Great Synthesizer: St. Thomas Aquinas
Greatest of the Greek Fathers: St. John Chrysostom
Hammer of the Arians: St. Hilary of Poitiers

Harp of the Holy Spirit: St. Ephraem (c. 306–73)
Illuminator, The: St. Gregory of Armenia (257–331)
Little Flower, The: St. Teresa of Lisieux (1873–97)
Maid of Orléans: St. Joan of Arc (1412–31)
Mellifluous Doctor: St. Bernard of Clairvaux (1090–1153)
Most Learned of His Day: St. Isidore of Seville (c. 560–636)
Oracle of the Church: St. Bernard of Clairvaux
Pope of the Eucharist: Pope St. Pius X (1835–1914)
Seraphic Doctor: St. Bonaventure (1221–74)
Spouse of Christ: St. Teresa of Ávila (1515–82)
The Theologian of the East: St. Gregory Nazianzen (c. 329–89)
Weeping Saint: St. Swithin (d. 862)

Latin Fathers of the Church

St. Ambrose, Bishop of Milan (340–97)
St. Augustine, Bishop of Hippo (354–430)
St. Benedict, father of Western monasticism (480–546)
St. Caesarius, Archbishop of Arles (470–543)
St. Celestine I, Pope (d. 432)
St. Cornelius, Pope (d. 253)
St. Cyprian, Bishop of Carthage (d. 258)
St. Damasus I, Pope (d. 384)
St. Dionysius, Pope (d. 268)
St. Ennodius, Bishop of Pavia (473–521)
St. Eucherius, Bishop of Lyons (d. 449)
St. Fulgentius, Bishop of Ruspe (468–533)

Greek Fathers of the Church

St. Andrew of Crete, Archbishop of Gortyna (660–740)
St. Archelaus, Bishop of Cascar (d. 282)
St. Astanasius Sinaita, monk (d. 700)

Saint Teresa of Lisieux

St. Athanasius, Archbishop of Alexandria (297–373)

St. Basil the Great, Archbishop of Caesarea (329–79)

St. Caesarius of Nanzianzan (329–69)

St. Clement of Alexandria, theologian (150–215)

St. Clement I of Rome, Pope (30–99)

St. Cyril, Bishop of Jerusalem (315–86)

St. Cyril, Patriarch of Alexandria (376–444)

St. Dionysius the Great, Archbishop of Alexandria (190–265)

St. Epiphanius, Bishop of Salamis (315–403)

St. Eustathius, Bishop of Antioch (d. 340)

St. Firmillian, Bishop of Caesarea (d. 268)

St. Germanus, Patriarch of Constantinople (634–733)

St. Gregory of Nanzianzan, Bishop of Sasima (329–89)

St. Gregory of Nyssa (330–95)

St. Gregory Thaumaturgus, Bishop of Neocaesarea (213–68)

St. Hippolytus, martyr (170–235)

St. Ignatius, Bishop of Antioch (35–107)

St. Isidore of Pelusium, abbot (360–450)

St. John Chrysostom, Patriarch of Constantinople (347–407)

St. John Climacus, monk (579–649)

St. John Damascene, defender of sacred images (675–749)

St. Julius I, Pope (d. 352)

St. Justin Martyr, apologist (100–65)

St. Leontius of Byzantium, theologian (sixth century)

St. Macarius the Great, monk (300–94)

St. Maximus, abbot and confessor (580–662)

St. Melito, Bishop of Sardis (d. 190)

St. Methodius, Bishop of Olympus (d. 311)

St. Nilus the Elder, priest and monk (d. 430)

St. Polycarp, Bishop of Smyrna (69–155)

St. Proclus, Patriarch of Constantinople (d. 446)

St. Serapion, Bishop of Thmuis (d.c. 370)

St. Sophronius, Patriarch of Jerusalem (560–638)

St. Theophilus, Bishop of Antioch (second century)

Doctors of the Church

Albert the Great (c. 1206–80); Dominican; Doctor Universalis
Alphonsus Liguori (1696–1787); Redemptorist
Ambrose (c. 340–97); Bishop of Milan
Anselm (1033–1109); Archbishop of Canterbury; Father of Scholasticism
Anthony of Padua (1195–1231); Franciscan; Evangelical Doctor
Athanasius (c. 297–373); Bishop of Alexandria; Father of Orthodoxy
Augustine (354–430); Bishop of Hippo; Doctor of Grace
Basil the Great (329–79); Cappadocian; Father of Eastern Monasticism
Bede the Venerable (c. 672–735); Benedictine; Father of English History
Bernard (1090–1153); Cistercian; Mellifluous Doctor
Bonaventure (1221–74); Franciscan; Seraphic Doctor
Catherine of Siena (1347–80); Dominican; second woman Doctor of Church
Cyril of Alexandria (c. 376–444); Patriarch of Alexandria
Cyril of Jerusalem (c. 315–86); Bishop of Jerusalem
Ephraem (c. 306–373); Deacon of Edessa; Harp of the Holy Spirit
Francis de Sales (1567–1622); Bishop of Geneva; Patron of Authors/Press
Gregory I, the Great (c. 540–604); Pope; Father of the Fathers
Gregory the Nazianzen (c. 329–89); Cappadocian; Theologian of the East
Hilary of Poitiers (c. 315–68); Bishop; Athanasius of the West
Isidore of Seville (560–636); Archbishop of Seville
Jerome (c. 342–420); Father of Biblical Science
John Chrysostom (c. 347–407); Bishop of Constantinople
John Damascene (c. 675–749); Monk; Last of the Greek Fathers
John of the Cross (1542–91); Doctor of Mystical Theology
Lawrence of Brindisi (1559–1619); Franciscan
Leo I, the Great (c. 400–61); Pope; Opposer of Heresy
Peter Canisius (1521–97); Jesuit; Second Apostle of Germany
Peter Chrysologus (c. 406–50); Bishop of Ravenna; Doctor of Homilies
Peter Damian (1001–72); Benedictine; Bishop of Ostia
Robert Bellarmine (1542–1621); Jesuit; Archbishop of Capua
Teresa of Ávila (1515–82); Discalced Carmelite; first woman Doctor
Thomas Aquinas (1125–74); Dominican; Angelic Doctor; Great Synthesizer

NOTES

Chapter 1

1. William Nicholas, *The Courage to Grow Old* (New York: Ballantine, 1989), p. 232.

Chapter 4

1. Phillip Berman, *The Search for Meaning* (New York: Ballantine, 1990), p. 352.

Chapter 6

1. Phillip Berman, *The Search for Meaning* (New York: Ballantine, 1990), p. 131.

Chapter 8

1. Francis Mleczko and George Bilecki are quoted in Patricia Treece's *A Man for Others*. Prow/Franciscan, 1994.

2. Maria Kolbe is quoted in Patricia Treece's *A Man for Others*. Prow/Franciscan, 1994.

ACKNOWLEDG-
MENTS

---

*I*n the course of writing this book, I have read many books on the history of the Church, saints, and spiritual development in general. I would particularly like to express my gratitude to the authors of the books I drew upon most heavily. In no specific order, they are: Alban Butler, for his classic, *Butler's Lives of the Saints* (Harper & Row, 1985); Brother David Steindl-Rast, whose book *Gratefulness: The Heart of Prayer* (Paulist Press, 1984), is must reading for any spiritual seeker; Father Thomas Keating, who taught me about Christian spirituality in his *Awakenings* (Crossroad, 1991); Henri Nouwen, author of *Reaching Out* (Image, 1975); and, finally Thomas Merton, whose book, *The Wisdom of the Desert* (New Directions, 1960) was most helpful to me while working on my chapter on the saints of the desert.

I would particularly like to thank my husband, Phillip Berman, who was greatly supportive of this effort from start to finish. I must also thank him, and his publisher, for giving me permission to quote from his books, *The Search for Meaning* (Ballantine, 1993) and *The Courage to Grow Old* (Ballantine, 1989).

Thanks must also go to the many museum reproduction departments in the United States and Europe who graciously gave me permission to use the many photographs that appear in this book. I would also like

to thank Larry Frank, author of *New Kingdom of Saints: Religous Art of New Mexico, 1780–1907,* and his publisher, Michael O'Shaughnessy from Red Crane Books in Santa Fe, for their gracious assistance, wit, and boundless sense of humor.

Finally, those of you who shared with me your many stories about the saints deserve a great deal more than thanks. While I was unable to print all of the stories you so graciously shared with me, your insights on the saints have both charmed and enriched me.

INDEX

About the Author

Anne Gordon grew up in Denver, Colorado, and graduated from the University of Denver in 1979. Winner of several awards for her writing, she has served as editor of the *Jackson Hole News,* assistant managing editor of the *Denver Post,* and assignment manager of KCNC-TV in Denver. She now resides in Cleveland, Ohio, where she is Sunday magazine editor of *The Plain Dealer.* In her spare time she enjoys sailing, bike riding, reading, and spending time with her son, Aaron, and husband, the author Phillip Berman.